BROKEN BUT BEAUTIFUL

Rebranding of a shattered Piece

Chioma Okoye

WestBow Press books may be ordered through booksellers or by contacting:

WestBow Press
A Division of Thomas Nelson & Zondervan
1663 Liberty Drive
Bloomington, IN 47403
www.westbowpress.com
844-714-3454

ISBN: 978-1-6642-5468-8 (sc)
ISBN: 978-1-6642-5470-1 (hc)
ISBN: 978-1-6642-5469-5 (e)

Library of Congress Control Number: 2022901790

Print information available on the last page.

WestBow Press rev. date: 06/08/2022

CONTENTS

ACKNOWLEDGMENTS

Without God, my guardian, my Father, and my friend, I would not have been able to write this book. His nurturing me and nudging me to constantly be the best version of myself has allowed me to grow and leap into an insurmountable amount of faith over the course of writing this book.

Also, I thank my husband, Ben Okoye, who allows me to spread my wings, and my family for their constant support; they instilled this vision in me.

I also thank my team for the consistent advice, editing, and patience it took to complete this project—my publishers; editors; my personal cheerleaders, the Deborah Praying Women—we have soared to the heights together, and this is just the beginning—and my special sister Margaret Effiom, who inspired me to finally start writing.

INTRODUCTION

> A wise one once wrote, "Don't despair if your heart has been through a lot of trauma. Sometimes that's how beautiful hearts are remade: they are shattered first."
>
> —Yasmin Mogahed

A *masterpiece* refers to a creation that has been given much critical praise and refining, especially when that creation is being prepared for a greater purpose beyond its understanding. During that period of metamorphosis, the creature possesses universality, artistry, permanence, and uniqueness. Spiritual and intellectual stimulation begins to mold the creature into its final form. Romans 8:19 (KJV) says "creature awaits the manifestation of the sons of God," and we are those creatures placed on earth by God, awaiting our own time of manifestation.

Likewise, in the spring, after months of hibernation and protection from the harsh winter, a flower finally begins to blossom. Throughout this book, I will document the wounds we go through in life's journey. One thing is sure: the pain does not disappear but must heal on its own. It cannot be rushed or forced. You may ask, "How we can heal with the eyes of the world seemingly staring at us?" Don't be ashamed of your scars; even Jesus Christ had his scars on display when the time came. At the core, *shame* is the shield so many of us try to hide behind. In our world, appearances matter—saving face, protecting your name and your family, asking yourself, "What will people think?" We must begin to see healing as a journey rather than a temporary mental fix.

I was deeply inspired by the words "broken but beautiful." After our annual conference centered on this topic, I decided to ruminate on it and turn it into more than a conference. It was during the process of developing it that the Lord revealed the biblical meaning to me. First comes *broken*—shattered and naked.

As a woman living in the twenty-first century, there is insurmountable pressure to conform through culture, especially in Africa, to our roles of mother, daughter, wife, friend, and sister to the best of our ability. We must bear the pain without fully understanding why we are going through it or how to come out on the other side. Expect answers in this book—real-life scenarios and people who will take us through their own personal journeys. This book will be your guide; hold it closely as you begin your journey through the harsh waters of change. Learn how to go through the deep waters and come out on the other side—broken but beautiful.

Writing a book was harder that I thought it would be but more rewarding than I could have ever imagined. None of this would have been possible without the love and support from my readers, motivators, and inspirators. When I began writing this book, I was going through metamorphic changes myself, both mentally and spiritually, so it is surreal that I have finally completed it.

For me, *broken* (shattered) is some sort of rebranding. Oh yes! It is a fact from my personal experience on my journey through life, which has transformed me into a brand this magnificent.

THE AWAKENING

I can't believe I am actually writing my thoughts and revelations after so many years of procrastination.

It was around four o'clock one winter morning when I woke up to a call about my father's death. I pretended I didn't hear what the caller was saying; I lived in denial for three days, refusing to believe it was true.

Accepting the truth was not easy. I passed through the stages of grief—depression, anger—why would God allow him to die after so many had said prayers—and then withdrawal. I was disconnected from everyone and everything. I went into my shell—until one faithful morning, as I was meditating, I heard the voice of God say to me, *"Do you know that before me, you are a broken but beautiful woman?"* I immediately sat up and stopped crying.

I felt so much joy and excitement, as if the Spirit of God had walked into the room to sit right beside me. I wanted to hear more, and I asked, "Really? Am I?" And I heard, *"Yes, you are."*

As I mentioned earlier, it felt like he was sitting beside me, smiling, and holding my hands. He then took me on a journey of recollection. I immediately remembered this quote from William P. Young in his novel *The Shack*:

> Pain has a way of clipping our wings and keeping us from being able to fly … and if [it is] left unresolved for very long, you can almost forget that you were ever created to fly in the first place.

What is the purpose of our creation: our happiness or God's glory?

> Do not be afraid, for am I in the place of God (Genesis 50:19 KJV)

Have you ever felt like you were all alone in life? Why do we have to go through so much as children of God?

1

Shattered

THE CREATIVE POTTERY

"Oh, wow, this is so beautiful," I said as I stared at the gold-plated design bowl, clearly love at first sight. I smiled softly and asked one of the sales attendants, "How much is this?" I was not fluent in English, but when he told me the price, I knew that what I had in my hand was worth every penny of the cost the salesperson had mentioned.

While walking around the tableware store for other choices, I realized that a particular section of the store was exclusively for beautiful crafted crackleware with different decorative patterns made of gold, silver, and platinum. I admired this spectacular section of the store and didn't even realize that I'd spoken aloud when I said, "These are unique and beautiful." My words caught the attention of another of the sales personnel. She smiled at me as though I was talking directly to her.

"Yes, ma'am, they are unique. They are actually made from broken or cracked ceramic tableware," She said with a bit of a Filipino accent. My face evidently showed my amazement, so she explained further. "The potter takes the original broken ceramic bowl or mug and fills its cracked surfaces with gold or silver powder, which transforms it from its original form into another design that becomes unique and valuable."

I was intrigued by this brief explanation, but I was imagining how ceramic tableware could have been damaged in the first place, before being transformed into all these masterpieces that were before my eyes. These beautiful and unique designs were worth any price.

As I walked up to the cashier to pay for my items, I spotted a decorative, well-crafted word-art frame with these words written on it: "In the midst of a crack, a beautiful light is created."

Immediately after seeing the blurb on the word-art frame, my mind was fixed on the cracked ceramic tableware, which had been shattered, but instead of someone disposing of it, that person had the idea for an exceptional masterpiece, a great signature piece that was valuable to the store.

As I was digesting this thought, the word *shattered* gave me exhilarating chills. Hmm!

Shattered is a word that gets me so excited every time I hear it or think of it. I know that it's a word that could bring pain to those who might have had emotional brokenness, but for me, it's a word that makes me appreciate that there is beauty within a cracked surface.

American educator and motivational speaker Yasmin Mogahed once said, "Don't despair if your heart has been through a lot of trauma. Sometimes that's how beautiful hearts are remade: they are shattered first."

Being broken (shattered), for me, is a type of rebranding. What do I mean by that? Here are the facts from my personal experience.

2

Growing in Tears

My visit to the Japanese art gallery, also known as the Japanese golden pottery, was an inspiring similarity to my reality as a broken piece.

My family time became a time of total submission. Bonded friendships became a path of misunderstanding. I had become a hermit because no one could understand or tag along on the new route that I was taking. It was a perfect life but, at the same time, it was a lonely one.

My rationale was to make that choice of having it all but, at the same time, clearing all. The core reason was the growth of transformation and remaking myself. As excruciating and hurtful as it could have been for me, I decided that I would remain on this journey. I also decided, after being inspired by the brief information about the unique pottery method from the sales person, that I would rather be recreated from my cracked pieces into a unique brand than become a brand that was discarded.

Again, my being broken is a type of rebranding. My personal experiences have transformed me into a brand that is magnificent. My rebranding has been a journey of growth that has wiped away tears; a journey of growth that has given me innumerable testimonies—this is not to brag; it's simply the truth.

On my first attempt at self-preservation during this journey, I thought, *This will be easy. I have friends. Gathering with friends shouldn't be a problem. I can adjust this time.* My being broken, however, was not based on my thought or self-belief that I was doing right or going down the right path. In addition to searching for more answers and directives as to what I was doing right or doing wrong, I was blessed to find myself in a transition that came as a revelation to me; it guided my understanding that the whole process of being shattered was a journey that was completely about me.

MY REVELATION TO COME HITHER

In a revelation from the Lord, I heard a voice say to me, "Come hither," and as I looked around, I saw myself on a mountaintop with many activities and attractions. Even with all that surrounded me, I still felt alone and in seclusion, which made me feel so lonely.

While on the top of my mountain, I experienced a sensation of deliverance. Afterward, a code was handed to me as a way to unlock a mystery.

As I blinked from reading through the code, I found myself in the midst of a congestion of back-and-forth movement; it caused pedestrian traffic to be in my way. Everyone seemed to be on the move at the same time. In a state of bewilderment, I decided to wait, as I didn't know where I was going or the cause of the mass movement and congestion.

I thought, *Moving past these people might put me on the fast track*, even though I didn't have a clue where they were going. I knew without a doubt that I had to stand there and wait for confirmation or approval to be forwarded to me.

While still on this quest, I suddenly realized that I was in a strange room. It seemed to be in a chalet, and it had my name written on it. On the side of the chalet was a specific note of instruction for an assignment.

I wandered around this rowdy but lonely place and noticed

people from different ethnic and racial backgrounds. Out of curiosity, I decided to search for a companion or at least locate people who were the same ethnicity as me so that I could mingle with them, even though I knew that searching for these people might waste the time that I needed for my given assignment.

While I was in the middle of following the instructions for my assignment, I still was deeply into a distracted search to find someone who had the same understanding as I had. I thought, *They will at least shine a light on all that surrounds me.* On the other hand, searching for someone with whom I could relate was at the expense of adhering to the timing of my assignment. Just as I was getting my thoughts in the direction of looking for someone to whom I could talk, I heard a voice say to me yet again, "Come hither to me," and then I woke up.

> Whoever gives heed to instruction prospers, and blessed is the one who trusts in the Lord. (Proverbs 16:20 NIV)

BEING AT THE RIGHT PACE

After my journey through this revelation, my heart had a constant message of "Come hither to me." I knew that this wasn't the regular status quo or within the current parameters of business as usual.

I knew that this was different from every other phase that I had been through, and although I knew that this wasn't within my comfort zone, I still thought I needed to upgrade my prayer life—I needed to be more serious in my spiritual life and should step up my pace.

As I had the notion of increasing my activities, it then dawned on me that this was deeper than making a to-do list with my cognizant mind—no, this wasn't the same. This was on a different level that stretched me more. It was a stage that expanded me more, where I would make more sacrifices. It was a point of being selfless more, escalating to higher heights; it was an altitude of edifying my capacity beyond the ordinary capacity with which I was comfortable.

It was like I was on a treadmill that goes back and forth on the same spot, with no sign of accelerated motion. I had to be picked up from that motionless spot and dropped on an isolated island, just to get the right pace.

I got to this point of seclusion as a result of experiencing much dysfunctionality. It was during this period of almost giving up that my memory clicked, and I saw who I was in the real world.

"Ah! Am I not Chioma, the principal of Diamond School of Etiquette and Protocol? I am a coach and a mentor. I groom people by molding them to excel through the instructive guide of rebranding." I said all of this out loud to myself, and had a reawakening in my mindset. This was when an idea came to my mind—it was rebranding.

3

Rebranding the Broken Pieces

Rebranding in the theoretical context is a state of self-discovery, self-understanding, or finding purpose. This can only be achieved by defining your destination, wrecking your old brand, and using the good wreckage with new schemes to create a more sophisticated brand that is unrecognizable from the former. With this, I knew that I couldn't afford to add toxicity to my new brand.

Following the rule of rebranding, I had to come to a place of will and affirmation to be wrecked (shattered) and enhanced, repudiating toxic people from the new evolution. With this new process, I understood that I needed the same pattern throughout my journey of spiritual rebranding.

In reality, this process happens in daily life around the world. For women, personal branding is a self-discovery of understanding themselves beyond what they have attained or have been through. The truth is that there is still more, and there is always a basis for being shattered in the first place.

I decided to add a twist to my professional life by following my own guidelines as a coach and a mentor. I knew that to get anything fixed or rebranded, it had to go through the hands of experts.

With a wide smile, I focused on the words that came through

to me during my revelation: "Come hither." I knew that I needed to be available to be fixed. In reality, as a rebranding expert, I always need the availability and willingness of my mentees or students to have a turning point in their lives.

It's always about the availability toward re-creation and rebranding. Just as there are basic guidelines of rebranding in the world of etiquette, I also saw myself with guidelines that encouraged my focus on being shattered. My understanding of the phrase "come hither" was that it unveiled a new form of service for me—a service that bore more pressure. It was a service of handling more responsibility; it was a service of being more knowledgeable.

"Come hither" was a journey with an attitude of overly excessive pressure. It was more of taking me to a place where relationships, friendships, and even my personal life would be relinquished.

"Come hither" led me to a vision of comprehending that misunderstandings would ensue, even from people I least expected, as they might think that I was too eccentric, over the edge, or doing too much, as they couldn't understand or catch up with the flow of the new fire outbreak, which I caught after being broken, which was beyond my control.

"Come hither" became my giving my all to God but at the expense of leaving my all, which included leaving friends, family, relatives, and staff, just to fully understand the term of being broken.

UNDERSTANDING THE FLOW

I compare being shattered with the tableware at the store, but the reality is that being shattered is a lonely journey. It's like understanding that the identity of a table decoration is basically different because its uniqueness is only attached to its different designs, and this understanding is similar to transformed cracked glassware, whose re-creation or renovation becomes a special golden piece but doesn't change its purpose of functionality as glassware.

Taking myself out of the circle of friends, family, and

acquaintances was definitely not from a point of malice or of ending verbal communication with them. Neither was it hostility nor aversion to them. There's a fallacy to the term *leaving them* as being physical abandonment.

This undefined separation was unavoidable, so no matter how hard I tried to continue in my comfort zone, my effort of trying to fit in wasn't working. Once I understood the essence of being shattered, I also understood that my calling was not a joke.

I just had to let go of trying to fit in or to convince anybody, even my closest friends. They couldn't just understand, so all I could do was put it in prayers. During this process in my journey, I created a habit of emphasizing the following:

> For God's gifts and his call are irrevocable.
> (Romans 11:29 NIV)

This scripture indulged my thinking that being shattered or broken is a calling, and it's a calling you can't alter, once you answer it.

It's a rebranding that is beyond the ordinary knowledge and process of renovating a damaged piece. It's about giving all of that dented item and turning it into a new piece, regardless of distractions or other attractions that may surround it. This is akin to my visit to the Japanese art gallery. With so much attractive merchandise, there was just something extraordinary and special about the cracked wares that were rebranded.

I believe that the potter would have seen other ceramics to polish, but he decided to use the broken ones for this unique rebranding purpose.

Even when you face the incredulity of your existence, you should take yourself back through the Genesis journey.

> So, God created man in His own image; in the image of God, He created him; male and female He created them. (Genesis 1:27 KJV)

As a reminder you need to grasp the purpose of your creation; you need to accept that you are a creation of royalty, and most broken pieces become the most beautiful pieces one could ever imagine.

A broken piece most often comes from a place of hopelessness, a place of bitterness. It could be emotional, physical, financial, or spiritual; it could be due to torn relationships, desires or expectations being cut off, or aspirations lost. It even could be people who have been emotionally crippled to a point of shutting down their entire minds.

The truth is, it's never an easy journey, regardless of the form of brokenness you have or encounter. But the good news I have for you is that I came from a place of spiritual and emotional brokenness. I was shattered. I was hurt, but I turned my wounded state into resilience. I knew that there was no better place for my being shattered and fixed than in Christ, rather than a place of being shattered and damaged completely.

From a sincere heart, I am telling you to keep persevering, and fix your mind on the prize—there is always beauty after a broken or shattered piece. Brokenness and beauty always work hand in hand.

Look at the story of Hannah. Hannah was a woman who was shattered emotionally, beyond words. She was in a place of bitterness. Imagine being mistaken for a drunken woman.

> Now Hannah spoke in her heart; only her lips moved, but her voice was not heard. Therefore, Eli thought she was drunk. (1 Samuel 1:13 KJV)

At this stage, words were beyond her, but her courage was beyond the world that failed her, for she knew there was someone who could fix her. She entered into her world of isolation and ran to the fixer to turn her bitterness into beauty.

> And she was in bitterness of soul, and prayed unto the Lord and wept sore. (1 Samuel 1:10 KJV)

4

Accepting the New Place

Once you have been shattered and rebranded as a Christian, you will recognize that the impact it gives you is the giving-all-and-accepting-all principle, as I would remind myself any time my mindset fell into a state of uncertainty or irresolution.

The truth about my journey is that when I decided, both by actions and by words, to give it my all, I got God's all. This is the same thing that happens to anyone who has fallen on this path called the shattered process. Once you give it your all, you will always get God's all. This could be getting his all in spiritual, financial, or emotional matters.

> Not that I have already obtained this or am already perfect, but I press on to make it my own, because Christ Jesus has made me his own. Brothers, I do not consider that I have made it my own. But one thing I do: forgetting what lies behind and straining forward to what lies ahead, I press on toward the goal for the prize of the upward call of God in Christ Jesus. (Philippians 3:12–14 NASB)

On the other hand, it's knowing that going higher is basically being on a flammable level of operation, and this new level may make it hard for most people to interact with you or be in sync with you. Their reasoning for your new flow or choice to go on a solo journey may be hard for them to comprehend.

When you understand being shattered, you understand that you have to fall into the realm of rebirth—this happened to me during my journey.

I had to go into hibernation to be in a place of rebirth in Christ, but it wasn't like the hibernation of a sleeping bear; it was hibernation that took me from the surface with which I was comfortable to a surface that God had decided for me.

GOODBYE, COMFORT ZONE

As humans, we generally accept that there is a method that translates our visions into reality, and such methods might be found in the people or particular groups with whom we associate. On the other hand, if we are fond of being a clingy type, then it might be tough to be ready for the new era of being shattered or rebranded, unless we become willing to accept the process ahead.

As I embarked on this journey, it was interesting for me to see myself dwindling to a place of total isolation because I was shattered, even though I had always had an attitude of confidence and strong social skills, coming from the profession of teaching etiquette and protocol.

The truth is, to be shattered is a journey that is based on falling away from a lot of things and associations. It's a journey that neutralizes your gregariousness and your comfort zone and replaces it with solitude.

I found myself in a stage-by-stage realm of solitude. One stage was separation, where I was physically around my friends and family yet felt disconnected from them. Another was the autocratic stage, where I was able to identify my directive of God's leadership in reference to the type of persons with whom I could or could not relate.

My profession of teaching etiquette and protocol put me in a workspace where I connected with different individuals and organizations. At this stage of autocracy, however, it wasn't "business as usual" for me because even my job and the type of people with whom I had to work were determined by God. It got so intense that I would wave off any person who wasn't in sync with how God was leading me, as it was all about God's approval at that juncture.

At that time, I was invited by a very influential dignitary to be one of the guest speakers at an annual international world conference. I knew the background of this conference, so I wasn't expecting anything less than the aristocrats who would be in attendance. While going through the program's itinerary, I came across the name of someone I had always wanted to meet, with regard to my profession. Thus, seeing this woman's name as one of the dignitaries made me very excited, as I knew that this would be an opportunity to eventually meet with her.

I was filled with excitement and felt this was what God wanted, so I accepted the invitation without hesitation.

"Oh, this is great," I said with a wide smile as I hung up the phone. Within a few seconds, I got a clear message within me that said, *Chioma, the theme you will be sharing on Thursday's house fellowship will be "Strength in Your Struggle."*

"Thursday!" I exclaimed aloud, as though I was conversing with someone physically present. I immediately checked my calendar to be sure that it wasn't less than two days after my upcoming international conference, as my travel routine was already used to having a two- or three-day interval. With this, I assumed that I would have that time or possibly would arrive on the day before the time of the fellowship, but this depended on the accuracy of my assumption.

Checking through my calendar, I realized that both meetings fell on the same date. With a deep sigh, I picked up my cell phone and texted my theme to a co-minister.

Just as I was about to confirm with a phone call that she had received my text message, I got another lucid message, with the echo of the word *you* said yet again. *Chioma, the theme* you *will share at Thursday's house fellowship is "Strength in Your Struggle."*

At this point, I dropped the phone on my desk and smiled.

There were years when I might have misunderstood this type of instruction and chosen whatever was self-pleasing, but with an attitude of yielding to God, I couldn't afford to question God or even ask further questions at that point, for all I had in me, at this stage of divine direction, was my obedience. With a clear understanding of his words, I knew I had to cancel the international world meeting so that I could be at the local meeting that was mandated by God.

> Jesus replied, "But even more blessed are all who hear the word of God and put it into practice." (Luke 11:28 NLT)

5

Depending Solely on His Leading

This level of obedience got me to a place of depending completely on God, a stage in which I trusted him absolutely. Reaching this stage of dependence was what connected me with the person I'd always wanted to meet; it gave me the best opportunity to meet and speak with her at the international conference, which I might not have attended, except for my following and heeding God's direction.

God always has a way of making the undoable doable, and it happens with such ease and with little work or effort.

Just few a weeks after my no-show at the international conference, I was connected to the same woman. She introduced herself to me, and after a little chitchat, a multinational deal was sealed within a forty-five-minute flight from Lagos to Abuja. Oh, halleluiah!

To understand this stage of dependency on the direction and guidance of God is to understand that God is too faithful to fail. It made me understand that nothing is *not* doable with God. It's a stage of knowing that following God's guidance can bring kings to the footstool of anyone who decides or is committed and dedicated to work alone by walking with God. I will always refer to such adoration as a *side-by-side walk with God.*

> And I will lead the blind in a way that they do not know, in paths that they have not known I will guide them. I will turn the darkness before them into light, the rough places into level ground. These are the things I do, and I do not forsake them. (Isaiah 42:16 ESV)

DIFFERENT ROUTE, DIFFERENT CALLING

> Don't be afraid of being different. Be afraid of being the same as everyone else.
>
> —unknown

Shattering is like confronting a bull. It's about doing something you ordinarily would not do, but then you see yourself doing it because it pleases God. It's a route on the map of God, even when it's a place you wouldn't normally go.

This phase is about having no choice, other than to trust God. It's normal for you to feel lonely on a journey with no outward security or a journey where there is no access to your comfort zone.

Feeling lonely is typical when God wants you to do things that are different from the things you usually do, but then, as humans of the Most High, we are uniquely made. God created each of us with matchless features, personality, and traits, and these exclusive attributes created the view of our differences, both in nature and in calling. No two fingerprints are the same; hence, we need to also understand that our calling and the level of how God chooses to employ us is completely different from what we might assume or expect after being shattered.

At times, what he tells you to do could be something you never could have imagined or hoped for. This could lead to a form of distrust, uncertainty, or numbness toward the world or all that surrounds you. You may feel that no one understands or relates to what you are going through.

This could be a reason for you to be lonely, but you may also wonder if it's only you—and you alone—who has been called to serve in the way God wants you to serve. It becomes a lonely journey, but when you understand the diverse uniqueness of your calling and journey, you'll have a rationale for comparisons or competition. At this point, you will have taken the lengthy route in this journey that makes your uniqueness different.

> In his grace, God has given us different gifts for doing certain things well. So, if God has given you the ability to prophesy, speak out with as much faith as God has given you. If your gift is serving others, serve them well. (Romans 12:6–8 NLT)

6

Broken Beyond Words

THE LEAP STAGE

We all need to take a leap of faith in the journey of life.

> When God pushes you to the edge of difficulty, trust him fully because two things can happen: either he'll catch you when you fall, or he will teach you how to fly. (Unknown)

My shattered journey wasn't a cushy one. No, it wasn't! It came to the point, after all the crooked corners of my journey, where I had to take a leap of faith, but the difference was that my leap was a beautiful one because of my total readiness for it. I understood my authenticity. I understood that there was a purpose. I understood my brand. And I understood that for my leap of faith to have a smooth landing, I had to trust and obey God.

You can't expect anything different from the norm if you aren't ready to trust and obey the instructions. This equation of "understand + trust + obey" applies even to our daily lives and activities.

TRUST AND OBEDIENCE ARE INTERTWINED

> God is Good, because He's God, He is worthy of my trust and obedience, I will find rest in no other than his holy will that is unspeakably beyond my largest notions of what He is up to. (Elizabeth Elliot)

Are you ready for the new phase after being shattered? Are you ready for your manifestation?

These were the questions I had to ask myself before I gave myself, all-in, to this divine leap stage.

Being broken is a submission to the ownership of Christ. Being broken is an intimate reflection on Christ. Being broken is beyond the physical; it's allowing God possess you with his Spirit, to use you for his will and for his good pleasure.

> For it is God which worketh in you both to will and to do of his good pleasure. (Philippians 2:13 KJV)

A COMBINATION OF ATTITUDE AND SPIRIT

An attendee at the Deborah Praying Women's annual conference, held in Lagos, Nigeria, asked me a question. Coincidentally, the theme for that year's conference was "Broken but Beautiful."

As she took the microphone from one of the ushers, she smile softly and said, "Please, woman of God, I would love to know if being broken falls on the notion of being a sinner, or if it is just a journey that should be only for sinners."

With a modest smile on my face, I thanked her for asking a vital question and immediately responded, "The truth about brokenness is that it's a method that God uses to deal with a self-focused life. When I refer to *self-focused life*, I am referring to the diverse personalities of everyone here. We are all born in the same way, but we all came into life with different characteristics. Because of our personal desires, we each act independently."

During a short recess, I looked for the young lady who had asked the question; she was seated in the conference room. As I made contact with her, I continued calmly, "Being broken by God does not necessarily fall on the sinful nature of a person or the sinful act of a person. Let's not misconstrue brokenness for repentance. One can be a Christian, yet not be broken."

Some Christians have a proud attitude and are obstinate or uncompromising in their natures.

I candidly will tell you that my shattered journey took place when I knew Christ, even after I had given my life to Christ, but I wasn't broken.

I became broken in my walk with Christ, and it was during this time that I was broken emotionally too. Being broken, most often, is not attached solely to the attributes of a person's spirituality or a person's attitude; it's the merger of a person's attitude and spirit.

The way you react to your children's behavior and their attitudes is also a typical example of how God operates with us when he breaks us.

You should not snap at children when their displayed attitudes are not good; you should focus on how to make them better by breaking their spirits to a form of instilled meekness and virtue, which will cultivate an attentive guide for them. The aim is that even when their attitudes push them to act inappropriately, their broken spirits will hold them in check. They will know that, at this point, they are being controlled by what you have instilled inside them.

The reality is that, as a parent, it's OK for you to let your children have their way sometimes, but it's never OK to allow them to have control over you.

Understand that it is only when you allow God be in control over you that you can know that you have fallen into a place of brokenness, which will pave the way for your spirit to be fully aligned with God and to flow with God.

> Very truly I tell you, unless a kernel of wheat falls to the ground and dies, it remains only a single seed. But if it dies, it produces many seeds. (John 12:24 NIV)

I summarized my answer to the attendee's question by saying, "Being broken by God is beyond being broken solely by personality or spirituality. Being broken by God involves the breaking of our will and our desires so we can experience our true breakthroughs."

CONTROLLED AND OVERSEEN SCRIPT

Being shattered is a form of liberating pride. It's a form of extricating a little rebellion here and there. It's a form of releasing ignorance, impatience, arrogance, and other qualities. Once you are able to release all these, then God will be in control of you, and he will turn all the cracks you once had into something precious and beautiful.

I heard a story about a certain man of God who committed suicide because his wife left him. Throughout their marriage, things were sweet and lovey-dovey with this couple, until the day he decided to follow the path of his calling into the Christian ministry.

Unfortunately, this was a problem for his wife, who strongly believed that she wasn't called to be a pastor's wife. For this reason, she indicated, verbally and by actions, that she wasn't going to support him and his ministry. She walked away from the marriage, which became a motive for the young man to take his own life. This was because he couldn't handle the shame and what people were saying about him.

The truth is that no manner how much love he had for his wife, it was not sufficient for him to have taken his own life. This type of act is an unadulterated sin of rebellion, pride, and what I call self-inflicted victimized mentality. You can never be broken and allow what the world says about you to control your emotions, actions, or thoughts. Only God has the final say, and once he is in possession of you, no egress or ingress of even the prettiest fairy will matter to you or to anyone who is really broken by God.

Being broken is allowing God to oversee you. At this point, you follow God's script, so no matter what, your excitement should be focused on getting it all back. Your excitement should be focused on knowing there is still more and there is a purpose. Therefore, you must focus your excitement on understanding your originality, which is your royalty.

Focus your excitement on understanding your brand as a person. The incredulity that you face regarding your existence should be a reason for you to take yourself back through the Genesis journey of knowing that your mark of royalty is based on the origin of your creation.

> So, God created man in His own image; in the image of God, He created him; male and female He created them. (Genesis 1:27 KJV)

As a reminder, you need to grasp the purpose of your creation as being God's own design. You need to accept that you are a creation of royalty. You need to appreciate that broken pieces can become the most beautiful design that one could ever imagine.

7

The Beauty That Lives Within

THE BEAUTIFUL ME THAT I NEVER SAW

As familiar as the word *beauty* may be to us, it's fair to say that a lot of people are more familiar with the outer definition of beauty.

THE HIDDEN MYSTERY.

One beautiful Saturday afternoon after lunch, I decided to take a short walk around the resort where I was vacationing. While walking around a beautiful park that was part of this resort, I spotted a peacock strolling along. Just after the bird passed me, it displayed its vibrant, spectacular colored feathers, with a rattle. At that point, I heard myself say, "Wow, you are such a beautiful creature."

This audible expression of my thoughts came with visible delight—the smile on my face. I could describe this bird was as a creature with an attractive beauty that is hidden.

A peacock, at first glance, is like other birds when its feathered tail is tucked in. You can only see this bird as a spectacular creature of God when it displays its vibrant colors.

The truth is, life is as beautiful as it sounds, and the beauty about life comes from the mystery of it. The hidden beauty about life could be similar to the air we breathe every second—no one has seen it, yet the beauty of it is its great importance to every living creature. No wonder that phrases such as "life is beautiful" seem so pleasant to the ear.

This saying from an unknown source captures it well: "The most beautiful things are always hidden."

A REFLECTIVE BEAUTY BEYOND THE PHYSICAL

Outer beauty is good, but there is always a greater beauty that comes with the epithet of royalty. This beauty is beyond sight; it's beyond the physical. It's more like a trace. It's a beauty that is revealed beyond the five senses. It's better defined by using the spiritual sense with a deep scrutiny of the true beauty possessed by someone who has been through a shattered phase.

During the shattered chapter in my life, it never occurred to me that I was broken to be a reflection of the beauty that basked within me.

My experience in the aftermath was like the scenario of the shattered ceramic tableware, which became a unique masterpiece, for its crack became the concept for the invention of a new design.

> God will take your broken pieces and use them to make you into something better, stronger and more wonderful. (Joel Osteen)

THE BEAUTY WITHIN IS A PLACE OF PREPARATION

The beauty within is a place of grooming or preparation. When a bride is getting ready for her wedding, she goes to a preparation room, where she does her makeup to enhance her physical appearance.

In most traditions, the assembled guests and the bridegroom don't see the bride until the ceremony. The admiration and praise given to the bride can only come after the unveiling, as one cannot make a rational judgment just from the process of her preparation.

The truth about such hidden beauty is that it comes from a place of service. People do not see all the hidden blemishes—sacrifices, pain, brokenness, hurt—or realize that is attached to success.

As a student, I never centered my preparation on the abracadabra method. Neither did I use a magic wand to reach this realm of inner beauty. It came from a place of brokenness, a place of being shattered, a place of rebirth. Most often, the reality of such an experience is that no one ever talks about, cares about, or knows the process, the suffering, the sacrifices, the heartbreak, the stewardship, or the labor that is behind the rebirth to such greatness.

The last time we hear about Jesus in the Bible is when he is twelve years old at the synagogue. Then—boom!—after eighteen years, when he is thirty years old, he resurfaces. I've always wondered about the path of his nonexistence throughout the eighteen years that he was not mentioned in the Bible.

Some people might base his resurfacing on the note about John the Baptist, who brought Jesus out through his sermon and narrative about the coming Messiah as a reason for his appearance at the river for his baptism. Upon meeting Jesus, John said, "I have need to be baptized of thee, and comest thou to me?" (Matthew 3:14 KJV).

I see the biblical season of the nonexistence of Jesus as the period when he went into hibernation, which would have been a time of preparation. The good news about such preparation is that he went into seclusion not just for himself but for humankind. That's why he is called the lamp of the world.

> When Jesus spoke again to the people, he said, "I am the light of the world. Whoever follows me will never walk in darkness, but will have the light of life." (John 8:12 NIV)

The beauty that is evident with the light that came with Jesus is that his preparation became that attraction, which became a game-changer for humankind. Its attraction and beauty ended all sorts of darkness for those who believe and are called, with an acceleration of victory over sin and death by giving us a place of luminosity and magnificent eternal glory.

My appreciation of the success story of Joseph in the Bible has always been that it was top notch. Imagine the story of a slave turned into the story of a ruler—and a ruler with no form of campaign. While reading through the scriptures (read Genesis 39–46), I noticed that the most emphasis on Joseph the great is attached to what he acquired as the vizier (prime minister) to Pharaoh in Egypt, rather than the deeper knowledge about what he actually went through before being given that position. Little is mentioned in the Bible about this time, but I believe there could have been seasons before his elevation to the position of vizier, where he might have starved for days. He probably would have been beaten, emotionally troubled, and the rest that we never read from the Bible story, apart from the time he was a slave, in prison, and was able to fight through temptation during his time of stewardship with Potiphar.

Joseph had to endure those times of persecution and torture, and that level of endurance was a preparation season for the manifestation of what God had bestowed upon him to come to reality.

His level of endurance and preparation was what made Joseph overcome the temptation and seduction by Potiphar's wife.

Imagine if it was otherwise and he had fallen to such temptation. I don't think he would have become known as the beauty of royalty and greatness that the world tags him to be.

I admire the success of great people, as I know they come to such an echelon of achievements that there would have been a stage of preparation that took much from them. Admiring the success of others is good, but we should also understand the stages they went through to achieve such success.

The process to greatness or the level of success as genuine Christians comes from a place of preparation, and this preparation comes from a heart and mind of deference. This act of deference only comes with intentional people. The ability to become an intentional person doesn't isn't from the act of prayers alone or the act of believing in prayers or prophesy. Belief cannot replace the hallmark of hard work and seriousness.

On the contrary, the ability to become an intentional person in this journey comes from the heart and mind of a hardworking and dedicated person who is set on attaining success. The unveiling of such success and beauty only happens with intense preparation; that is why, most times, such preparation is beyond the physical. The beauty of a house is only revealed after its finishing point, but before getting to that point of perfection, there was planning and cost estimates and all the rest.

When we first got our first home, I nodded my head most of the time, although I barely understood the architectural plan or drawing sheet that the architect brought to me. It didn't make sense to me, and I was only concerned about the completion of our home. I never appreciated or saw the beauty of all the planning and the foundational structure, not until the house was completely built.

On the other hand, the architect already had a full picture of what he was building, even before it was completed. The day I visited the site after the final painting of the house, the first words that popped out of my mouth were, "This is beautiful!" I was only able to see and appreciate its beauty after completion. That scenario reminds me of why I refer to God as the architect of my life.

During my shattered days, I never knew that I would be transformed into the Christlike beauty that I am today. Even with all the uncertainties that would revolve around me, the Architect (God) who started the work in me already saw the beauty within me before it was completed. This result came from understanding and trusting God, with the help of the Holy Spirit, when he said to me, "Come hither." He alone knew the level and height of his plan.

THE BEAUTY OF AN ATTRACTIVE FRUIT

This type of beauty is linked with that of a sprouted seed that evolves into an attractive fruit or beautiful flower.

The process of planting a seed can be messy, but the messiness isn't that attraction. The attraction is for the outcome—the fruit—that evolves from the buried seed.

I became a beauty in the eye of the beholder (God), and my attraction was like that of a fruit.

> But let your adorning be the hidden person of the heart with the imperishable beauty of a gentle and quiet spirit, which in God's sight is very precious. (1 Peter 1:4 KJV)

My being a shattered piece was what forged me into this beauty that is beyond the physical. The whole essence of that shattered journey was that I should use it to bless others.

> The generous man [is a source of blessing and] shall be prosperous and enriched, and he who waters will himself be watered [reaping the generosity he has sown]. (Proverbs 11:25 AMP)

In another context, your experience has to be a blessing to someone; otherwise, you will not see that beauty within.

Someone once said, "There is nothing more beautiful than someone who goes out of their way to make life beautiful for others."

The whole essence of your inner beauty should be an impact or a blessing to others.

The beauty of a woman is not in a facial mole, but true beauty in a woman is reflected in her soul. It is the caring that she lovingly gives, the passion that she knows.

—Audrey Hepburn

8

The Beauty of an Attractive Fruit

The reality of a seed is that no amount of packaging will prevent the seed from dying when it's buried in the soil because the beauty of any fruit is from the product of its decay.

I related to the significance of this, as I defined my rebranded beauty as a beauty that's in the eye of the beholder (God), and my attraction and beauty is like that of a fruit that spreads its harvest in its season.

BLESSING OTHERS WITH A BEAUTY WITHIN

You cannot be endowed with an honorable gift but selfishly choose to keep all to yourself. The beauty within is like the beauty of a sprouted fruit—its primary purpose is its harvest so that it can be consumed by others. Imagine how ridiculous it would be for a farmer to go through the planting season, then harvest the fruits, but then decide to store the fruits all for himself.

In reality, no matter how much he might try to consume all the harvested fruit himself, he surely would not be able to eat all of it. Understand that the beauty within you is for the purpose of exploring. Use that beauty as a form of blessing to others so that they also can experience the type of grace that you have been privileged to experience. As previously mentioned, the essence of your inner beauty should be to impact or to be a blessing to others.

FUNCTIONING WITH PURPOSE

The beautiful me that I never saw had to deal with change. I had to be on standby, in the guise of spiritual hibernation, for my reinvention.

This time, I was at a completely different level—an observant level toward my reinvention,

I looked beyond the physical. I looked beyond what I saw in the mirror. It was more like a reflection beyond the surface. It was a deeper view. It was more of a concave scrutiny; it was an inward observation.

Then a thoughtful question popped to my mind: "What's your level of functionality?"

With the effect I had gotten from my reinvention, it was easy for me to lay out my answers to this question.

For me to function with purpose, I needed to pause, to be on standby.

For me to function with purpose, I needed a big change, a win-win change.

For me to function with purpose, I had to fall into a place of hibernation. (Once you are hibernated, you are ready for reinvention.)

Every process I took to unearth my beauty within was worth it. It's a beautiful thing to be in the grip of God's hallmark. If you have not yet had this grip of God's standard, then please recalibrate inwardly, and you will see beyond the physical.

To understand your purpose, ask yourself this: "What suits me? Where's my place with God?"

Once you have an answer to those questions, then your

experience will become your currency, where there are no impediments.

Discovering your beauty within is attached to your purpose on earth, which brings about true knowledge of who you are.

It is a confidence-builder, and you will reap the merit of fulfilment for yourself and the God who created you.

Once you identify with this type of beauty, you can never be short on contentment. You will encounter an end to consternation, complaints, and competitions, as you will now be grounded with confidence, insight, and intuition. At this time, your peak in livelihood, creativity, re-creating, discerning, multiplying, and fulfilling will become automatically of royalty, like your Father in heaven.

> Whoever says he abides in him ought to walk in the same way in which he walked. (1 John 2:6 ESV)

Your beauty within is a place of resurfacing. You will definitely stop existing and start living the purposeful life of your rebirth. Your life at this rebirth will become a life where it's no longer the directive of your voice but a place where all that is heard is God's voice.

9

His Voice

> So, as the Holy Spirit says: "Today, if you hear his voice."
>
> —Hebrews 3:7 NIV

HIS VOICE

Hearing the voice of God is important to our existence, whether it's by his inner witness of the Holy Spirit or through the Word of God.

Our Lord Jesus said:

> To him the porter openeth; and the sheep hear his voice: and he calleth his own sheep by name, and leadeth them out.
>
> And when he putteth forth his own sheep, he goeth before them, and the sheep follow him: for they know his voice.
>
> And a stranger will they not follow, but will flee from him: for they know not the voice of strangers. (John 10:3–5 KJV)

When we hear the voice of the Shepherd, we are not misled. We will not stray from the path he has set before us; we will not be deceived by the "stranger," and we will fulfil our God-ordained destiny.

Sometimes, we need to be silent or practice quietness to allow the voice of our Shepherd to be louder than our voices.

HEEDING THE MASTER'S VOICE.

Heeding God's voice is in the vein of a servant heeding the voice of his master. In most homes with servants, there will be one or two servants who are loyal to the voice of their master, even to the extent of risking everything to be obedient. At my relatives' home, I once witnessed one of the stewards disobeying the instruction of his madam, all because he had to be loyal to his master. This was a funny episode to me. My personal judgment of this was that this young man's deliberate action came as an acknowledgment that his master's voice was superior to the voice of his madam, regardless of the fact that she was the head of the household—it's normal in my culture for women to have the higher rank in the household.

I jokingly asked the steward, "What will you do if your madam says you are fired for this act of disobedience?"

His response held so much confidence: "My master will defend me because I did the right thing by obeying him."

This young man's response brought me to an imaginary conclusion about the realistic behavior of humans when it comes to loyalty and trust. The confidence in the young man's response was from a place of trust he held for his master. His deemed legitimacy toward his service to his master would only have come from a place of belief and from the authenticity of loyalty from an obedient servant.

> Servants, obey in all things your masters according to the flesh; not with eyeservice, as men pleasers; but in singleness of heart, fearing God.
> (Colossians 3:22 KJV)

I related this experience to my journey as a child of God, which cascades on the conduit to my confidence in God's voice, rather than my own conduit to my personal comfort zone. Heeding God's voice is the summit of total submission. It's a point of neglecting what could happen or what might not happen, even in the midst of any risk or inconvenience that might affect you as a person.

While I was seated on the sofa, I thought that, in reality, that genuine act of obedience that this loyal young servant displayed toward his master could have cost him his job, but his decision was to regard the voice of his master, regardless of his disobeying anyone else. It was his call of loyalty; for him, that was the best thing he could have done as a servant who understood the importance of his call of service.

Heeding God's voice goes beyond respect; it's about the acknowledgement of your Master's title. It's about diligence toward his being Lord. As a child of God and as a human being, I know that diligence to stewardship is about productivity. It's a display of God's character in you, and it's an action toward obeying everything that God says you should do, even to the point of hearing what he says you should do through his heartbeat.

Following and obeying God diligently is knowing that every other thing will be added unto to you. Similar to the story of the loyal steward, we should understand that obedience to the voice of God, at all times, comes with a reward.

> Now it shall be, if you diligently listen to and obey the voice of the Lord your God, being careful to do all of His commandments which I am commanding you today, the Lord your God will set you high above all the nations of the earth.
>
> All these blessings will come upon you and overtake you if you pay attention to the voice of the Lord your God. (Deuteronomy 28:1–2 AMP)

As much as life has its ups and downs, I would tell you from the sincerity of my heart that one of the greatest simplicities as a Christian is heeding God's voice, which could be through our dreams, revelations, visions, and so on. It's all about the way we project our minds as genuine children of God or Christians.

This precedent is a way to steer every child of God who has been through the reinvention process to understand that all that matters is making the voice of God your flesh. Once you have made the voice your flesh, it will begin to nudge your gift, to a point of understanding that the voice of God and even the Word of God is everything in your everyday life. Understanding this is understanding that not even the tiniest manipulation of the voice from anyone else or even your own voice matters, once the voice of God has spoken or given a command.

DEFERENCE TO HIS VOICE IS BEYOND THE NORM

In the past, I have subconsciously, consciously, and even unconsciously been put on the spot of heeding my own voice. Some people would refer to it in Nigerian slang as the "I-know-too-much attitude." Most times, such an attitude results in meekness in the long run.

The day I stopped trying to be ahead of God's voice was the day I realized I had missed out on a lot of things he had to teach me, a lot of things he had in place for me. Thank God for the restoration gift!

Don't get me wrong; I always was an obedient student who knew Christ, but realistically, there are times when a student will be late on assignments, or will choose to do them later. The student might choose to be over the edge but still will get the response of "No, that's not correct" from the teacher. Realistically, you cannot be the best student if you are one who talks ahead of your teacher or if you aren't quiet and heedful while being taught. Remember that a well-exhibited practical is as a sequel of your attentiveness and compliance to the theory. Thank God for my shattered tour!

Regardless of your place or what height you have attained, there's a time when odds could fail you. It could be in your daily endeavors, relationships, spirituality, and so forth. A sincere search of this could be due to your obduracy to listen to God—and it's not just about listening to him but being 100 percent obedient to his voice.

Deference to God's voice is a point of understanding your voice, to where you have been groomed by God. It's a point of consecration to the voice of patience and to the voice of the Holy Spirit.

Imagine God telling you, "I need you to go up to Madam A and apologize for her acting cruelly to you."

I would bet that 99.9 percent of the persons in that position would disobey God and affirm their inner voices. Well, God's ways can never be our ways, so I won't push further on the outcome to such disobedience.

> For my thoughts are not your thoughts, neither are your ways my ways, says the Lord. (Isaiah 55:8 KJV)

THE GIFTED REWARD FROM OBEDIENCE

There is always that place of preparation for you as a Christian that is not divided in service or fellowship. This preparation is also a place of purpose, and this purpose is an act of being able to actualize your dreams. It's a place of having the knowledge of what it takes for your dream to manifest. One of my lessons during this journey was learning that there is a difference between the kingdom gift and the gift that comes as a reward for obedience. My understanding is that not everything from the kingdom is a gift. It's as eccentric as understanding that not every tummy rumble is a symptom of hunger. The fact is that some gifts that we possess as Christians are as a reward for our obedience.

A minster of God once shared a testimony, in which he said that when he became fully aligned in obedience with the purpose and instruction of God's voice, he became blessed with the gift of interpreting his dreams,

"Of course, I had always had that gift of dreaming. I would wake up and the picture of the dream would be there in details, but I never understood what it meant—until the day I was instructed to follow a path that was not pleasing to me or to men. My dear brethren, that was the day I began to experience, in depth, the gift that came as a reward for my obedience. Since then, no dream of mine comes without a clear interpretation."

Listening to the testimony of this minister of God gave me more clarity about the gift that comes from obedience and the gift that we are blessed with from birth. It connected with my personal journey, which was on the subject that some gifts are from obedience.

10

A Confirmed Journey

The journey of life is filled with challenges. Some are the normal daily challenges that are quite common with all humans. Some are like mountains. Some are swampy and overwhelming, which might seem insuperable. It's at such a juncture in life for the believer or the student of Christ that the knowledge and the ways of God prove useful and become an enormous courage booster. A reprimanding word from the apostle Peter says,

> Grow in the grace, and knowledge of our Lord and Savior Jesus Christ. (2 Peter 3:18 NIV)

Having the knowledge and understanding of God and his voice implies having an awareness of what God says he can do, wants to do, and will do at his will.

> I have spoken, and I will bring it to pass; I have purposed, and I will do it. (Isaiah 46:11b ESV)

The level of understanding God's nature, voice, and will does not just fall into our laps. It's a perpetual process of walking with God and abiding his holy written word. This magnitude is shutting down completely and making God the innermost voice that always speaks to you. Know with assurance that this can be one of the smartest things you can do for God and for yourself.

Do you know that listening and conforming to God's voice can make him turn any betrayal to a form of rebranding and blessing for you? Imagine your enemies becoming as easy as bread for you, all because you listened to the voice of God.

> Only do not rebel against the LORD, nor fear the people of the land, for they are our bread; their protection has departed from them, and the LORD is with us. Do not fear them. (Numbers 14:9 KJV)

Imagine your enemies coming in this way and fleeing the other for the purpose of this passivity to the voice of God.

> The LORD will cause the enemies who rise up against you to be defeated before you; they will come out against you one way, but flee before you seven ways. (Deuteronomy 28:7 AMP)

Being in awe of God is assured victory, regardless of which battlefield you may be in. He did it for Jonathan, he did it for Gideon, and he did it for so many people.

> One man of you shall put to flight a thousand, for it is the Lord your God Who fights for you, as He promised you. (Joshua 23:10 AMPC)

Holding your peace is all you need to do. By just saying his word as a confirmation of your trust for him, you will be assured of peace on all sides, for in God's voice remains possibility!

THE CLARITY OF GOD BECOMES THAT POSSIBILITY

The intelligibility of God is understanding his transparency; it's understanding his precision to plan and execute his words, regardless of the barriers ahead.

Understanding God to be your voice is to know that once you speak in reference to his Word, he confirms your voice and makes the impossible possible.

Having the type of clarity that Jonathan had about God is a great thing. Imagine going ahead in the midst of thousands of huge and powerful men with spears, knives, body armor, and probably guns and still not feeling intimidated. Instead of intimidation, he went ahead to instill his faith and confidence about God into his armor-bearer, who was the only person with him to face these men.

> Jonathan said to his young armor-bearer, "Come on, let's go over to the fort of these uncircumcised men. Maybe the LORD will act on our behalf. After all, nothing can stop the LORD from saving, whether there are many soldiers or few. (1 Samuel 14:6 CEB)

Can you imagine such clarity and faith combined? This was the type of assured clarity that Jonathan, the son of King Saul and the crown prince of old, had of God. If I were to draft Jonathan's words of faith and confidence in my version, it would be thus:

Whichever side of the divide you fall into, numbers mean little or nothing to God.

The truth about God is that once you have clarity about who he is, you will have a constant understanding about his voice or Word by just blending your faith with it. This was the lesson God passed to Gideon by finally telling him to go into the battlefield with only three hundred men against an ally of nations.

Gideon's character in the Bible is shown as a man of valor (as called by God) and with a heroic nature, but Gideon perceived fear. Who wouldn't be afraid of facing a whole nation with just three hundred men in his army? But when Gideon was in doubt, God stirred up his voice in him, and it was more like, "I am boss, my friend. Stand up and gather three hundred of your men to fight."

God doesn't approve what he has not said. Once he has approved or said something, he will confirm it through actions. That was why Gideon, in no manner, was able to disobey God, for God had the final say.

A similar lesson is found in the story of Samson, the popular one-man army. Samson wouldn't have been able to put his confidence in God if he hadn't had an intimate knowledge of the God he served.

Samson was a strong man, from his birth to his death. Do you know what it means to kill the all the Philistines with just one blow, as Samson did? I am sure even the greatest boxers would be shocked!

But Samson wasn't afraid to ask God for that type of impossible thing because he had the knowledge that his God was a divine splendor. His clarity about God was so sharp that even in his blurry physical state, he still trusted God for ferocious strength to destroy the Philistines. Hallelujah!

> Then Samson called to the LORD, saying, "O Lord God, remember me, I pray! Strengthen me, I pray, just this once, O God, that I may with one blow take vengeance on the Philistines for my two eyes!" (Judges 16:28 KJV)

What does this tell us? God's voice is a wonder. I feel so excited when imagining the shock on the faces of the Philistines.

FAITH IN GOD'S WORD IS THE WAY TO GO

It was the genuine faith that Samson had in God that wrapped up his action.

> But without faith it is impossible to please him: for he that cometh to God must believe that he is, and that he is a rewarder of them that diligently seek him. (Hebrews 11:6 KJV)

Not all types of faith please God. What is overlooked in all this is that faith is good only when it engages truth. Remember that the Word of God is true. When faith is made to rest upon falsehood, it often does lead to eternal greed.

It is not enough to believe a thing; it's all about believing the right thing about the right one (God). Believe in God, and believe that his voice is more than believing that he exists. Aha! Judas believed that.

True faith requires believing everything that God has said about himself but also what he has said about us. Until we believe that we are as bad as God says we are, we will never believe that he will do for us what he says he will do.

Manipulation of the scriptures to have a quick way out or have an unjust compliment and consolation is as good as despising the written word and rejecting the living Word, which is a verification of vanity. Trusting and heeding God's voice means trusting his actions. It's trusting that God can never be man. It's trusting his authenticity.

Clarity about God is focused on averting lack, meagerness (insufficiency), lack of strength, and situations that may seem impossible and looking up to the almighty God. Looking up to God is listening and obeying his voice. Once you are fully dedicated to the voice of God, victory is certain against whatever your own voice or the voice of man proclaimed was stronger than you.

> What shall we then say to these things? If God be for us, who can be against us? He that spared not his own Son, but delivered him up for us all, how shall he not with him also freely give us all things? (Romans 8:31–32 KJV)

His voice is steadfast for us. His voice is paying attention to us. His voice knows what's best for us. His voice is perfection.

> The value of persistent prayer is not that God will hear us but that we will finally hear God.
>
> —William McGill

As people after God's heart, you and I desire to please God (obedience) and to be aligned with his voice (will). Receiving the fulfillment and peace that we desire is based on our obedience to what he actually wants.

Life, sometimes as cruel as it could be, could turn in a different direction from our expectations, even after a shattered and remolding phase, and you wonder, "Am I on the right track? Is this who I ought to be or where I ought to go? Am I going in the direction God would have me be?"

Often, the outward knowledge of God's voice and the persistence to hear his voice can be scary and doubtful. But having an altruistic attitude toward God's voice and all he asks us to do is worth everything. This type of attitude and obedience is a conduit to a more purposeful, powerful life and is mostly pleasurable to God.

Listen to Jesus, who said, "This voice was for your benefit, not mine" (John 12:30 NLT).

Imagine the Son of God knowing that the voice of God is for our benefit. Is this not enough to make us understand that no matter what we say, the talk now until years from now is and will be all about the voice of God.

11

At the Foot of the Cross

MY WORSHIP! MY ENCOUNTER! MY SACRIFICE!

Oh, how I love the song "My Worship" by Phil Thompson. Part of the lyrics are:

> You Lord, You are worthy
> And no one can worship You for me
> For all the things You've done for me
> And no one can worship You for me

Truly, no one but me, myself alone, can worship God for me,

> An encounter with God marks you and makes you hungry for more of him. (Jenn Johnson)

Once you have made worship your quiescent space, you will understand that worship should be part of your encounter with God.

God deserves our worship, whether we are in a place of hopelessness, sterility, or disorientation. Turn your every stitch to worship.

> How do you know when God is at the center of your life? When God is at the center, you worship. When God is not, you worry. (Rick Warren)

Worship is great when it becomes your experience.
Worship is great when it becomes a thing of the heart.
Worship is great when it becomes true.
Worship is great when it becomes a sacrifice.
And to whom this great worship is due is the greatest.

> Wherefore we receiving a kingdom which cannot be moved, let us have grace, whereby we may serve God acceptably with reverence and godly fear. (Hebrews 12:28 KJV)

I know a lot of Christians speak of worship as an activity where hands are raised, eyes are shut, heads are lifted or bowed, and songs of worship are rendered. Well, the reverence, the adoration, the lifting up of hands with closed eyes and singing songs, and calling God various names are still part of worship, but until your worship is in sync with the depth of your heart and soul, then it's not your encounter.

Worship is something that no one can execute for you. True worship is an endearment; it's a deep, devoted feeling that can only be understood inwardly by you, even before expressing it. It's a spiritual affection that outwits our five natural senses.

> God is a Spirit: and they that worship him must worship him in spirit and in truth. (John 4:24 KJV)

I have learned to use my mode of glorification (worship) toward God as a lifestyle—a lifestyle without a component of culture to it, not even the culture that emulates my daily living of things that surround me or the culture that simplifies my basic needs and wealth.

We should adapt this lifestyle by making it a mode of worship that reflects the condition that is all about the goodness of God, not the goodness or riches that life has given to us.

> Worship is no longer worship when it reflects the culture around us more than the Christ within us. (A. W. Tozer)

BEING AN EXCEPTIONAL WORSHIPER

Gideon in the Bible taught me how to worship God in an exceptional way, beyond what might surround me.

Gideon worshipped God, even with all that surrounded him. He got down on his knees, and he worshipped. He gave his whole heart to referencing God at a time when he would have been gearing up for the physical battle that was ahead of him. Instead, he got on his knees, which meant that he understood that victory in the battle was his yielding to the one who can defeat even the mightiest army. With this understanding, his focus, after having a dream (see Judges 7:15), was to worship God. Gideon worshipped God from the depth of his heart. He worshipped God in advance for a victory that he had not seen yet.

Gideon was known for having exchanges and dialogue with God, and in all of these conversations, Gideon always asked for something from God. The day came, however, when he had to express a display of worship, and of all days that Gideon could have used to ask God for victory and protection, he decided to worship God.

Gideon got down on his knees. He didn't request anything from God, not even the strength to slay the army. All he did was drop to his knees, lift his face and his hands toward God, and say to God (in my own interpretation of this reverence in worship), "Lord, I don't know how this battle will end, but I am going to worship. Any way that this battle will end, I am going to worship. I am worshipping you, Lord, in anticipation that you the one who started a good work in me. Regardless of where this battle will lead me, I will bring it to completion."

Gideon, from the depths of his soul, worshipped God in advance. (See Judges 7–8:22.)

The ample blessings we receive and the answered prayers are great reasons to testify, but it shouldn't be a reason to worship God.

It is very easy to worship God during the good times, but we need to learn how to make our worship a reference that God is magnificent.

I remember a conference that we had with the theme "True Worship." In one of the testimonies, a widow spoke of losing her husband to the cruel hands of death, and she had children to feed, family on her case, and other issues.

Life became horrific for her. At some point, hope was lost, but in the midst of these trials, she developed a passion for God, where worship was what she had going. Inexplicably, her worship experience was that quantum leap (breakthrough) and healing for her and her children. Her worship became the robust experience she needed to win the fierce battle against hurt, pain, and struggles.

During her testimony, even the song she sang as her form of worship would have been understood only by spiritually bonded persons, for the realm this woman was in was deeper than what we heard or saw.

> Worship is an act of war against the enemy of our hearts.
>
> —Holley Gerth

12

My Essence of Worship

Oh, how I love the psalmist called David. He was a man who had the brand of worship I am talking about.

He had a different type of worship that I defined as the "four parts of worship" that one should have as a true worshipper.

The first worship I associate with David had all the worship one could assimilate, if true worship were to be copied—the *worship of totality.*

> And David danced before the LORD with all his might. And David was wearing a linen ephod. (2 Samuel 6:14 KJV)

This type of totality means that there was no holding back, and David worshipped God with all of his being.

The second worship I associate with the character of King David is worship that portrays contempt.

> Michal, the daughter of Saul, came out to meet David and said, 'How the king of Israel honoured himself today, uncovering himself today before the eyes of his servants' female servants, as one of

> the vulgar fellows shamelessly uncovers himself!' (2 Samuel 6:20 ESV)

This type of worship is a typical example of my kind of worship. I don't notice what other people say or think about me during my time of worship. Ironically, if my worship involves my somersaulting for God, I sure will do a somersault.

Disgust or contempt from anyone with regard to my conduct during worship never has a hold on me. To whom I render my worship is all that matters to me. I can imagine the impact of the worship that would cause a king to strip naked during his worship, which made the queen say he was a shameless man. Where David was, however, it was an acceleration of glory. This type of expressive worship would make one appear dense in the eyes of others, but in the eyes of God, it is as a sweet aroma filled with holy words.

During one of my exaltation sessions in the Deborah Praying Women online fellowship, the sermon's theme that day was "The Priceless Value of Knowing God." A particular highlight during this hour was that I became totally committed to God. And just before the prayer session, I was led to ask everyone to turn on their microphones and sing a song of worship of their choice, individually, to God at the same time.

Normally, it was difficult for everyone to sing or talk with the same rhythm during an online meeting, due to the delay in audio, which caused a draggy sound. This was adequate reason to be discouraged from singing together. We had an online tradition of muting microphones while one of the musicians led a single worship session.

With all this, I had to encourage everyone to participate by reminding them that the value of knowing God was about the commitment that we, as children of God, give to Him. Once they were able to focus their worship on God, he automatically became the center of worship, making it impossible for anything—even the draggy, echo sound—to distract them.

With this message as motivation, the atmosphere was charged with different songs and a flow of worship. I, on the other hand, was so deep in my own worshipping that I didn't pay attention to who was singing this or that. I also didn't pay attention to myself, so I didn't know that my network was disconnected temporarily, not until I got a call from the technical team, telling me they couldn't hear me anymore. I just started laughing, and while waiting for my system to reconnect, I told myself, "My worship is all about God."

This type of worship is the third part to the type of worship that King David expressed, which is a worship that is centered on God.

Having this type of worship is like having an I-don't-care attitude. It's like telling the world, "I don't care if I'm the greatest or worst singer or dancer or clapper. I don't care if my bowing in the eyes of the world isn't the right thing. I don't care if I have to be in rags. I don't care, for my heart is directed to God; my worship belongs to God, who is the center of my worship. All I do and how I do it is before the one who deserves all of my worship." Our worship doesn't have to be constrained by our self-consciousness or the awareness of others.

> And David said to Michal, "It was before the LORD." (2 Samuel 6:21 ESV)

True worship is an encounter in which you literally leave your body and are connected fully in spirit and soul; it's a deeper root of adoration. It's beyond the five senses or the physical. It's more like a transcendence. It's a spiritual contact and connection to our adoration of God and not to things visible or human. This is the type of worship that King David had; it was a Worship of unending intimacy, a worship of growing deeper.

> I will make myself yet more contemptible than this, and I will be abased in your eyes. But by the female servants of whom you have spoken, by them I shall be held in honor." (2 Samuel 6:22. ESV)

"I will make myself yet more contemptible," he said. It's all about growing deeper. I delight, just like David, in growing deeper in expressiveness, deeper in articulating a heart filled with adoration and gratitude to God.

GOD DESERVES ALL ADORATION

Making worship a lifestyle is the simplest when you give your affection and respect to God by directing all your love and adoration to him.

Once you are able to do this, then nothing visible will matter at that time. Your career won't matter, your spouse won't matter, your hobby won't matter, the challenges of life won't matter. For me, even this book I am writing won't matter, once I am in that realm called *true worship* because the flow is blind to anything visible. All adoration is only connected to the King of kings and Lord of lords.

> O come, let us adore him
> O come, let us adore him
> O come, let us adore him
> Christ the Lord
>
> —"O Come, All Ye Faithful"

Music is sweet, and voices are divine, but understand that all those are like camouflage in the sight of God in reference to worship. What God is particular about is the quality of our hearts.

CASTING ALL FOR HIS PURPOSE.

When I am in worship mode, I cast aside all other agendas for this purpose. What could be more important than a time of true worship that is focused on God?

What makes worship so treacly is the extravagant expression

and the stillness. It's like a trance of sweetness, where so many of the melodic tunes of intimacy can only be understood by you in expression to God.

I have been through this type of worship, and I must tell you that my trust in God has deepened. Sometimes, I am overwhelmed with things, and confusion and restlessness set in. Once I embellish my worship with a little bit of prayer, the rest becomes a mood of gratitude.

Even when there is fear of an unknown future, never relent in trusting God. Trusting God is the hope of tomorrow. Our worship must have a greater effect by making everything within us become *that* worship to God. When there is any sort of a blink, remember that we are called to fulfill his purpose.

If, at any point in time, you come to a phase when you are at a dead end, forgetting that your calling is for his purpose and not your own, please remember the reason for this fulfilled purpose.

I have seen people take turns in performing the "rumble" form of worship—the type of worship in which people roll from one corner to another—but they come back to a place of spiritual ignorance, which is obviously a form of disobedience to the life they claim to have. A couple of these types of ignorant worshippers have asked why my life was different and why things worked differently for me. My response was simply, "I am God's purpose."

> Worship the Lord in the splendor of his holiness;
> tremble before him, all the earth. (Psalm 96:9 NIV)

DEEPER THAN THE DEEP

Once your heart has learned to behold the beloved, and once your heart has learned the growth that comes with the awareness of gratitude, then you will have that *deep call unto deep encounter* that expressly desires the renewal of God's presence.

We could kneel or stand; we could lie low or high; we could

shut or open our eyes; we could lip sync, sing, or be in silence. We could be in the gathering of saints. We could be in a marketplace or alone amid folks, with music or no music, lyrics or no lyrics. Worship is a heart posture that is deeper than the deep.

13

Restoring Dignity

UNDERESTIMATING THE HAUL FROM THE DEPTHS OF THE OCEAN

Glancing through the sun's flickering from the window of my terrace, my mind went down memory lane, reminiscing on my childhood days and how I was so appreciative. I am someone whose appreciation level has always been high; this attitude was part of my upbringing. Hence, imagine the gratitude I had every time I received a gift.

Yet I underestimated one gift that was given to me as a child. I had no knowledge of its worth or value, but it became a basic precept for me as I grew older, after understanding that it was a precious gift.

As humans, we tend to fall short on gratitude worthy of boasting. We are cajoled to fall prey to the guise of underestimation, all because we might be ignorant or lack understanding of what we are blessed with and privileged to have as a gift. This same attitude comes explosively into our lives as Christians, as we get into a phase where our mindset is that waves are a creation from the pull of the wind to the surface, when actually, it's a force from its depth that pulls the waves to the surface, coming from the deepest part of the ocean.

A PRECIOUS GIFT UNKNOWN

My dad would bring me gifts for no special reason almost every time he came home. Those gifts always reassured me that I belonged and was loved. These gifts from my father were special to me, as I believed that I was the apple of his eye.

I woke up one pleasant morning, with the typical morning hellos and compliments in our home.

I heard Dad call, "Makalisa?"

"Yes, Dad?" I responded, blushing, with a smile on my fair face—this was in response to the name he was fond of calling me, which is translated as "the most beautiful one."

With a glow of affection on his face, he said, "I need you to take a ride with me somewhere."

Without hesitation, I hopped into the car, as it was always a pleasure to accompany my dad to functions and places, as I was his buddy.

Driving down the clay road with my dad, I could see an expression of pride on his face. In a soft tone, he said, "Omalicha [meaning "precious one"], do you know that you are wonderfully made?"

Without a second thought, I replied, "Yes, Dad," with so much confidence in my voice. I didn't know why he had asked the question or what tie the question had with the place to which we were heading.

Just as I was about to verbalize my thoughts, my dad parked the car by the side of the road, "Oh yeah, we are here," he said with a mild giggle.

I sluggishly got out of the car.

"Please hold on to this Gunter's chain for me. We need to get an accurate landmark, OK?" he said.

I responded with a nod and followed his direction.

After a long process of marking out plot by plot, he smiled at me and pressed his hands together, as if to applaud me. "Thank you, my dear daughter. You did a fantastic job."

I smiled and blushed. "You're welcome, Dad."

AN UNKNOWLEDGEABLE VALUE

At our next stop, although I believed we were finished, my dad walked back and forth on the measured site. It didn't surprise me to see him reconfirm the measurements, as he was, by nature, a very careful and precise man.

"You did an excellent job, my daughter," he said with his thumbs up. "I must commend you, and I have a gift for you."

I was so excited and wondered what the gift was. I walked swiftly toward the car, anticipating that my gift was there.

Then my dad said, "All this land I give to you as an inheritance, my dear child."

My initial inward feeling was disappointment, as I was expecting a feminine, more valued gift, which was what I was used to. Who would blame a child of such tender age for feeling that way? I didn't understand the cultural role that was attached to daughters inheriting landed property from their fathers. This was a gift to which I paid no attention—at least, I gave it less importance than other gifts, as I didn't know its value or its worth as a child. It wasn't until I grew older that I understood the importance attached—by culture and by people, especially my own tribe—to a female child inheriting landed property from her father in those days.

Still strolling down memory lane, the word *dignity* popped into my head. Knowing God in the way I know him, I knew that this had to do with him. As I thought about the word, I only understood the theoretical definition of dignity, defined as "the state or quality of being worthy of honor or respect."

A QUESTION FIXED

Wandering through my mind was another thought: *What happened to the word dignity?* This question took me into a deeper realm with the Holy Spirit. This rumination took me through the book of Genesis, also known as the book of creation. As I was scrolling through the spiritual understanding of dignity, my mind went back to my childhood, when my dad gifted me with a landed property. Clearly revealed was that the word *dignity* came from our heavenly Father and that many people never understand its value or worth. This was similar to my not understanding the worth or value of the gift from my dad. Knowing Christianity in the way I have been blessed to understand, it's an encounter of growth. We all grow, and usually it's through this growth that our eyes and vision of understanding grows. Imagine being awarded a gift so precious and priceless that it was the reason for the devil to steal it originally through the revenue of sin.

I took a sip from my teacup as I studied the book of Genesis, and I developed my thoughts and understanding about the word and the role that dignity had to play with humankind. Just then, there was a knock on my door. It was my steward, who had come to tell me that the electrical technician had fixed the electrical problems. Being my usual self, I bluntly said, "I hope he checked the problems very well."

"Yes, ma'am," he responded.

I smiled at another discovery; this was in relation to the word *fix*. Without a doubt, I knew that my comment to my steward about fixing the electrical issue was a further glimpse into the realm I was in.

Realistically, it was unfeasible for anyone to fix, repair, or restore anything or anyone without having knowledge of the background fault. As I continued reading the book of Genesis, it hit me that our first parents, Adam and Eve, were actually the originators for the dignity of humanity, which was ripped off in the first place, making them the background fault.

14

Wonderfully Made

Sinking deeper into the realm where that I found myself with the Holy Spirit, I remembered my dad's words when I was as a child, telling me that I was "wonderfully made." That phrase clued me in to the importance of my dignity, and I remembered the scriptures in the song of Psalms that gave a confirmation of the existence of the wondrous creation of my nature. I decided to profess it over and over again, as an affirmation of my purpose.

> I praise you because I am fearfully and wonderfully made, your works are wonderful, I know that full well. (Psalm 139:14 NIV)

To be *wonderfully made* brings something extra to your creation. It's having those unique components in you that is so extraordinary. God is a unique spiritual being, and from the commencement of creation, he attached his unique gift to humankind, as a result of our creation, by making us heir to his honorable, unique nature, which is in his image and likeness.

Obviously, this unique gift of dignity caused the anger and jealousy of the devil. He then decided to take it out on humankind in a plot to steal our dignified legacy by making our first parents his prey; he caused them to sin under the guise of knowledge, which was actually the root of disobedience. This act of sin was also the reason for the initial disconnection from God, due to their disobedience, which was the fountainhead of sin to the world.

Sin was the very setup the enemy used as a technique to diminish the dignity of humankind, marring our dignity as human creatures.

A GIFT ROBBED THROUGH SIN

Before sin: "And they were both naked, the man and his wife, and were not ashamed" (Genesis 2:25 KJV).

After sin: "And the eyes of them both were opened, and they knew that they were naked; and they sewed fig leaves together, and made themselves aprons" (Genesis 3:7 KJV).

This knowledge was the sin of disobedience to God, and this sin was what cut us off from our dignity.

I imagined this type of destructive knowledge with just one bite of an apple—but my imagination hadn't gone far when the Holy Spirit put me in check. It made so much sense to me that without the sin of Adam and Eve, there would have been nothing to fix; hence, there wouldn't have been a need for restoration.

I realized that distinguished dignity is on a higher level and obviously is far different from the definition the English gurus set it to be.

Dignity is a confirmed gift from our heavenly Father, and it became a gift to the human race right from our first parents, Adam and Eve.

Imagine a complimentary gift of royalty, free of charge, with no stipulation of racial background or skin color, no stipulation of financial or marital status or any sort of status as a prerequisite to be a recipient. This reminded me of the words my dad used to describe me: *priceless gift*! I understood clearly that dignity, in its own, was that gift to humankind, without a price. I knew that dignity is a gift awarded to and deserving to be received by all equally.

A GIFT RESTORED THROUGH CHRIST

Once I got deeper into the understanding to which the Holy Spirit guided me, I channeled my thoughts about dignity toward the present and not the past (where I was with Christ before I was shattered). My realization came with an understanding that the eruption of our dignity from the origin of our first parents through sin became the good news to our present state, which became the divine glorification through the disposition of restoration.

> Nevertheless, death reigned from Adam to Moses, even over them that had not sinned after the similitude of Adam's transgression, who is the figure of him that was to come. (Romans 5:14 KJV)

This restoration came through Christ, and even though the actions of Adam and Eve removed our dignity, God still loved us so much that he gave us his only Son, so that our dignity that was taken would be restored, hence making us new creatures.

> For God so loved the world that he gave his one and only Son, that whoever believes in him shall not perish but have eternal life. (John 3:16 NIV)

I took a quick peep at the television screen. I was tuned to one of the foreign news channels, which was reporting on people, both young and old, who were on a protest mission in a popular country. The televised protest got to me, as all I could relate with was the chaos due to a failed system.

While watching the television, I didn't even realize I was angrily charged up, but I said aloud, "It wouldn't have come to this if there was a system that valued its citizens equally!"

ELEVATING HOPE THROUGH RESTORATION

Almost immediately, I turned off the television and picked up my phone to have a conversation with a relative who lived in that country. I wanted to be sure that my relative was OK and well.

As we were talking on the phone, I realized that it is essential for us, as humans, to know that the role for the modern dissection of the scripture is a guideline opportunity for us, as Christians, to contextualize the gospel into our real lives. It charges us to take hold of the revealed inner messages of hope, and it aids in giving us a perfect mode of conduct as dignified persons by matching the biblical principle and standards; hence; we know that our lives are portrayed with values, even in our broad lifestyles in general.

The essence of my TV time made me understand that human dignity is something often ignored by many systems and structures, if not all. Most of this ignorance can be applied to our modern society, which seeks to understand and restore a positive life and relationship. Instead, it often becomes nonviable as the system fails to meet these obligations.

Imagine the lives that would have been lost, all for the notion of wanting a system to understand and honor their request and value.

This might sound dreamlike, but the truth is that I have always looked up to the gospel for indulgence that will elevate hope on the whole of this journey, sailing through the past disappointing experiences of life. It is a reminder that Jesus's restoring lives is for grace and dignity, which no human or system can evaluate.

ASSIMILATING YOUR DIGNITY LEVEL

Dignity is fragile, and it's a natural characteristic for all human creatures. On the other hand, I see dignity as fluid because it's a gift that God allowed to flow with ease to us. That's why God dignified humankind from creation.

Dignity is the state of being worthy of honor and respect.

Dignity is attached to our moral rectitude, and this is correlated to our behavior.

When your state of mind is on the right path, you will be able to muster the moral characteristics or luxurious self-indulgence (decadence) that will justify the dignity gifted to you by God, who is the Father of all good and beautiful things.

> Every good gift and every perfect gift is from above, and cometh down from the Father of lights, with whom is no variableness, neither shadow of turning. (James 1:17 KJV)

Once you are able to understand the expectations and characteristics of dignity, your mindset as a mother, father, husband, pastor, evangelist, wife, daughter, son, man, or woman will always be appropriate. Your state of mind will always be linked with your actions. I can never relinquish the moral decadence that works with the role of dignity when the mind is not in sync with the actions.

One of the training courses on etiquette that was organized by the Diamond School of Etiquette and Protocol, of which I am the founder and principal, was on etymology. All trainees were asked to wear a particular type of outfit. which was to imitate the theme for the practical training.

I noticed one of the trainees wore completely different attire than would have been expected for a formal British tea party, as hilarious as it was to the other trainees. When she walked in with a traditional African head tie and a very different pattern of costume, I didn't take her seriously, just based on her appearance.

As a rebranding coach and fashionable person, I know that the way we dress is partly a description of the world's view of us, our disposition, and orientation of our character. Fashion, on its own, has a way of decoding the hidden personal attributes of humans.

Imagine being a role model to someone, but your comportment differs from the character you portrayed originally. I would say such an individual does not deserve the true honor that should be accorded to a role model or mentor.

My days of restoration came as a function of bringing me back to the former position, but this time, I became molded to my position with the functionality of Christ in me, who became the ransom for my restored dignity, which is embedded in the image of God.

> So, God created mankind in his own image, in the image of God he created them; male and female he created them. (Genesis 1:27 NIV)

I love to keep reminding myself that I am wonderfully and powerfully a replica of God's image. Our creation as humans was branded with respect and dominancy. That's why the Bible captions our creation with the image and likeness of God. We are made in the image of Christ so our self-worth is rooted in Christ, regardless of what took place decades ago in the garden of Eden, when we were robbed of our dignity, an outcome of the disobedience of humankind that eroded our rightful place. But thank God for Christ, who came to reposition and restore what was lost.

15

Fear Not and Take Back Your Position

As I was taking a walk and chatting with my daughter on a cold, windy evening, a thunder clap came from the sky.

"Mummy, let's go back," my daughter said. "We didn't come with an umbrella or phone, and we might get wet once the rain starts."

I looked at her with pursed lips and said, "We will finish this walk."

Turning around, I could see fear on her face, even though she mumbled, "OK, Mum."

Of course, I didn't know if we would get soaked by the rain, or if the rain would meet us there or halfway. All I could sense was my confidence in my words to my daughter. This type of confidence was an assurance for both of us. It was a confidence that was filled with boldness. I could have decided to run the way that others were running, but I was calm and kept walking, as if the clouds were sane.

The way I brag about my faith as God's own comes even to the smallest of things. I can never allow fear or turbulence take hold of my position in Christ. I always have that zeal of charging myself, even when others are fretting.

I don't have time for nonsense that tries to spark fear in me. We kept walking, as it was part of our workout routine, and we eventually got to the house. Immediately as we stepped foot into the house, a heavy downpour started.

My daughter looked at me with a sigh of relief and said, "Mum, did you hold the rain till we finished our walk?"

This question got me laughing until tears came to my eyes. I told her, "My darling, once you know in whose image you are made, not even the wind or lack of a means of communication will put you to fear. What you see now is evidence that I know my position in Christ, and Christ, at that time, would have said, 'Child, be still.' So I knew the wind would be still until the daughter of the Most High finished her walk. Laughing, I went to freshen up.

I always use everything I go through in life as self-motivation. I don't see any need for anyone who understands God at the same level that I do to be relentless in any form, regardless of what may come their way or seem to be turbulence or obstacles. Always keep in mind that our places have been rebranded with Christ, for he came as a means of restoration for us. Why should we fear when we know where our position lies? It's time to fear not and take charge of your position.

> And I will bring my people Israel back from exile. "They will rebuild the ruined cities and live in them. They will plant vineyards and drink their wine; they will make gardens and eat their fruit." (Amos 9:14 NIV)

The confidence level of our first parents was at zero. That was why they allowed a guileful serpent to convince them that what God said about the fruit was not true.

Confidence is a fear- and gibberish-chaser. Having confidence is standing as firm as a rock that can never be moved by anything you say or anything you believe in. Once you confidently grasp the gift that you have, you will comprehend why the devil found a way to attack that gift called dignity.

The enemy's organized networks, or organized intimidation, which has subjected so many humans to a life of depression, low self-worth, anxiety, and fear, shouldn't be a reason for fear. You need to charge yourself with the laudable fact that you deserve to have it all and have it to the brim, regardless of how the devil tries to raid your physical, social, psychological, emotional, and even your spiritual sense of worth. Know that Christ has restored you to the fullest.

> The thief comes only to steal and kill and destroy; I have come that they may have life, and have it to the full. (John 10:10 NIV)

It's important to understand the full package and the archetypal design with which you were created from the onset of creation.

One of my major instruments in life is awareness. It's one of the tools that has brought me to where I am now and where I am going. To be victorious or up-and-coming, make *knowledge* one of your paramount tools.

Knowledge is power; hence, it's of utmost importance for you to understand your origin. Understand the species you were created to be and whose image you are representing as a person and as a child of God. Knowledge and comprehension are critical to winning mental battles by intentionally strategizing a structural defeat in the warfare of life.

> For our struggle is not against flesh and blood [contending only with physical opponents], but against the rulers, against the powers, against the world forces of this [present] darkness, against the spiritual forces of wickedness in the heavenly (supernatural) places. (Ephesians 6:12 AMP)

> For God has not given us a spirit of fear and timidity, but of power, love, and self-discipline. (2 Timothy 1:7 NLT)

BE ENLIGHTENED AND FEAR NOT

During one of my study sessions, I came across the word *deilia*. Initially, I pronounced it as *Delilah* until Google taught me the correct pronunciation, which is "day-*lee*-ah." Deilia is a Greek word, translated as "fear" and sometimes defined as "timidity or cowardice."

> Fear not, for I am with you; be not dismayed, for I am your God; I will strengthen you, I will help you, I will uphold you with my righteous right hand. (Isaiah 41:10 ESV)

God's gift does not function well if we are too apprehensive to use it. You can only use the gift of dignity when you are fearless. It's important to understand that his gift has power, love, and "sound mind," just as 2 Timothy 1:7 has emphasized.

In my search for more knowledge, I had learned that the phrase "fear not" is used at least eighty times in the Bible.

What if this phrase "fear not" is actually a command from God? I thought.

> Don't fear, for I have redeemed you; I have called you by name; you are Mine. (Isaiah 43:1 CEB)

"Don't fear, for I have redeemed you." Ah! Another scripture that uses that same phrase—"fear not"! For this phrase to occur over and over again shows that God knows that the enemy uses fear to intimidate us and to seek to diminish our aspirations and limit our victories. It's a mandatory wake-up call for us to understand that fear of any sort should not have a hold on us.

Being frantic is unrealistic for anyone who has been through the shattered process, as I have, or anyone who understands the purpose of the gift of dignity. Why should one be terrified? Why should one fear? There should not be room for thoughts or beliefs that allow the enemy to intimidate you.

Was it a practical joke when God said he gave us a spirit of sound mind and not a spirit of timidity? No, he meant it! I like the sound of the Greek word for fear, deilia. With assurance and guarantees, no one should subject themselves to deilia, unless there is something fundamentally wrong.

16

All for His Mercy

In as much as God laid out the consequences for the rebellious act that was committed by Adam and Eve (see Genesis 3:9–16), my enlightenment about his judgment toward them was that God was still able to swaddle them before sending them out from the place of plenitude, which was part of their punishment. As a coach, I study and interact with different types of people on a daily basis. I know who people are; we tend to forgive by mere words and not by actions.

Imagine this rebellious act as being a twisted form of human-to-human interface. What you would get might sound like this: "Adam and Eve, you rebelled against me, your boss. That's fine. I forgive you. You can go."

Adam and Eve would be happy and take what they could. Then, while stepping out from the gate, they would get a reaction like this: "You dare not touch anything. Make sure you return all the food and leave the clothes I gave you. Just take yourselves out the way you came, and make sure you don't call me because I have blocked your number!"

I'll bet that many people fit into this illustration. But even in the midst of the rebellion, God was still able to care for Adam and

Eve before evicting them from the garden of Eden. Even after they left, he was still there for them.

Isn't this a pure observation from the scriptures—that God is merciful?

Let's always understand that punishment differs from hatred. Punishment retribution or discipline. In the case of Adam and Eve, God had to send them away from their comfort zone of abundance, which was the garden of Eden, to a place of toiling, which was the consequence for their actions of breaking their rooted covenant, a price for the withdrawal of our original dignity.

Mercy, mercy, mercy! Where would we be without the mercy of God? Two of my favorite scriptures are as follows:

> It is of the LORD's mercies that we are not consumed, because his compassions fail not. (Lamentations 3:22 KJV)

> I will have mercy on whom I have mercy, and I will have compassion on whom I have compassion. (Romans 9:15 NIV)

It's by the mercy of God that Christ came through as the restoration for us and as a divine platform for us to regain our dignity. Therefore, we should rise to our full potential, knowing that Jesus has us covered.

> Everything the enemy has stolen, God is going to restore to you: the joy, the peace, the health, the dreams [house]. (Joel Osteen)

THE PLACE FOR DELIVERANCE AND RECONCILIATION IS THE CALL OF TRUTH

Remembering God's call to Adam in the garden gave me more understanding about the reason why God sent his Son to us. Even when Adam and Eve found out they were naked and then hid, God still made that call. It was a call for deliverance; it was a call to restore order, regardless of the offense that Adam and Eve committed. It was a call that said, "Hey, child, stop hiding and get your act together. I know what you and the woman I gave to you did." It was a call of reality (truth).

No wonder Jesus presented himself as the way, the truth, and the light. He knew that his restoration for us had to do with our deliverance from the bondage of intimidation and deception, which had played in our minds from inception. We can have no greater form of liberation for our minds than the acceptance of the call of truth.

> Then you will know the truth, and the truth will set you free. (John 8:32 NIV)

There was a time in my life when my knowledge of Christ was good. I would do things and feel that I had done enough. I remember the day when I realized that I was just playing by going in a different direction from the purpose to which God had called me. It was like going in a direction of self-convenience, and it kept going on, until the day that I realized, "Ah, this is disobedience."

I cautioned myself; no one had to tell me what to do next. I went to a place where I knew that all I needed was for God alone to pick me up. It was a place of reconciliation, a place of consecration. The reality is that, most times, the deliverance we need is all about a reconnection with God.

It's not about trying to make peace with God; it's about being at peace with God and being justified by faith through our Lord Jesus Christ. Once you are at peace with God, your heart and mind will be guarded, causing the peace of God inside you to become the peace of God outside you and in all your affairs.

KNOWING THE DIFFERENCE.

Oppression and inferiority are never from God. They are a result of sin; they are a form of guilt. Once you stride on the right path and perceive the light of this glorious gospel, then you will be free from oppression and inferiority.

> Come, descendants of Jacob let us walk in the light of the Lord. (Isaiah 5:2 NIV)

Have you been oppressed by the old mindset? Have you struggled with feelings of inferiority?

If you have been a victim of oppression or inferiority, it's necessary to change in your mindset. You are made in the image and likeness of God; hence, you need to renew your mind. This renewal is having the function of Christ in you.

I personally believe that any dignified person in the body of Christ needs to be enlightened and aware of how the enemy tries to swindle us and how God wants us to maneuver.

HE BECAME A REASON FOR AN END

Remembering the words of my papa, "priceless gift," gives me so much joy. I know that this confirmation also came from God himself, who is my superior Papa.

This optimistic feeling of knowing my place with God also stands as an affirmation that our restoration is the reason Jesus went to the cross, that the cross is the reason he lived again, and that the life in him put an end to everything that was natural from the Adamic race. Hallelujah! This is one of the reasons that I can stand at my balcony window every morning, look up to the sky, and boldly declare, "I am priceless because Christ paid the price for me!"

> For the Son of Man came to seek and save those who are lost. (Luke 19:10 NLT)

There is the joyful and exciting feeling of knowing that our restoration was an end to sickness, an end to penury, an end to defeat, an end to ache, an end to curses, and an end to sin and death.

There is cheerfulness in knowing that all that was natural ceased to be in the life of Jesus on the cross and was all that was supernaturally constant in him. And the joyous privilege of being priceless is because Christ decided to put that life in us so that we could regain our dignity, knowing that *the life of Christ became that reason for restoration!*

Oh, hear this! Jesus rose from the dead so that his life would be added to the power of resurrection, hence depositing his resurrected life in us—the life of Christ is in us. Let's pick up the pace and come out of the shadows by operating in the light, for we have been given dominion over the earth to maintain it, to care for it, and to nurture it and everything in it.

Always remember that this authority and dominion is not based on our gender but is totally based on our belief and acceptance of God Almighty. The enemy tricked Adam and Eve out of that authority, but Jesus restored it to us.

> But that is not the way you learned Christ!—assuming that you have heard about him and were taught in him, as the truth is in Jesus, to put off your old self, which belongs to your former manner of life and is corrupt through deceitful desires, and to be renewed in the spirit of your minds, and to put on the new self, created after the likeness of God in true righteousness and holiness. (Ephesians 4:20–24 ESV)

17

The Voice of Betrayal

Being an etiquette and rebranding expert has been a platform with which I have associated myself in helping many individuals of different ethnicities, different genders, different ages, and different backgrounds.

One beautiful morning, while getting ready for work, I glanced in the mirror to check myself out, which is my regular routine. "Who is this gorgeous being? You're so fly. You're so beautiful," I said to myself.

Later, as I walked onto the office premises, I noticed one of my employees standing with a young woman; they seemed to be involved in an altercation.

As a professional and as an expert, I find it inappropriate for anyone to make a scene in the workplace, regardless of their status. With a soft smile on my face, I walked past them, believing they would notice me and then would tone down their voices.

When I got to my office, however, I noticed that the volume of the squabble had increased. I knew I had to take steps, regardless of the personal inconvenience, to try to relieve the situation.

Once I got to them, my employee, who understood my mood, immediately became calm.

As an expert in emotional intelligence and behavioral

management, I smiled at the young woman and said softly, "Good morning, miss. Please, I just need you to understand—"

The young lady, without hesitation, interrupted my sentence. "Understand what? Understand what?" she lashed out at me.

I apologized to her and walked away.

My job has taught me a lot about managing and dealing tolerantly with people. Most times, I believe that this was what God ordained for me to do professionally.

YOUR ROLE IS AN ACT FOR THE IMAGE YOU REFLECT

I went back to my office, leaving security to professionally take care of the altercation. I eased into the chair at my office desk and opened a Bible, which is part of my daily obligation before I begin any training session or work task. Flipping through the scriptures, I glanced at a page that read:

> And we all, with unveiled face, beholding the glory of the Lord, are being transformed into the same image from one degree of glory to another. For this comes from the Lord who is the Spirit. (2 Corinthians 3:18 ESV)

I sat still in amazement and satisfaction of what I'd just read! "I am the reflection of God's image," I told myself. "I choose to be a manifestation of God's glory. Wow! I see God's glory every day in the mirror, and now I understand why I am fearfully and wonderfully made." I giggled ecstatically at my own words.

The words I spoke to myself took me back to the incident that just had happened at my workplace and the way that the young lady had spoken to me. I imagined the repercussions if my reaction had been different or if, without a second thought, I had reacted in the same way as she had reacted to me. I knew who I was and knew my brand, and I couldn't have been pushed to such a repugnant level of action and character. Ironically, I couldn't have been pushed to the level of becoming repulsive because my mirror didn't endorse that at all.

You can't be a mentor or a coach and allow yourself to be manipulated by the behavior of your mentees. Under no circumstances should you allow their character or behavior to change you. Always have it at the back of your consciousness that once students walk into your discipline, it is your obligation to make sure that they progress from your discipline or mentorship as replicas of what they have learned.

Your mentees should be reflections of you as their mentor. It's absurd that a soccer coach would train players for the purpose of soccer, yet on the pitch, players would display the skills for snooker. That's never heard of or done.

In the flow of the amazement that came with the scripture in 2 Corinthians 3:18, I thought back to part of God's creation and how he tagged humankind to his own image when he said, *This is my image.*

> So, God created man in his own image, in the image God he created him; male and female he created them. (Genesis 1:27 ESV)

Being in God's image means that you need to be his replica, his duplicate copy. This copy is beyond the physical copy; it's more of how you express God, not just through your words but through your actions.

I mentor my mentees on etiquette, protocol, rebranding, and other courses on emotional intelligence, but no matter what I say as their mentor, if it's not echoed in their actions or practices, then there is nothing to show for what they were taught. With that, going out in public as a brand or representative of Diamond School of Etiquette and Protocol is totally inconceivable.

Being a reflection of God is affiliating yourself with God's view. It's a display and manifestation of God's characteristics.

18

Reflecting His Glory

Each day when I get dressed, I go to the mirror to check my appearance. Once I am pleased with what I see, I set out on my day. If I'm not pleased with what I see, I add accessories or change my outfit until I'm satisfied. I believe most women practice this routine activity every day.

The mirror reflects and reveals my image, giving me a view of myself, although the image that is revealed doesn't define me.

> Everything in your life is a reflection of a choice you have made, if you want a difference result, make a different choice. (Unknown)

Now the similarity between a mirror's reflection and God's reflection is only with the word: *reflection*. God's reflection is about God and not about any human attributes. It's about God's appeasement and not the satisfaction of humans, including me. It's about displaying and manifesting God's image through his characteristics in obedience to his Word. The reflection from the mirror can only give you what you see at that time, but it cannot define you. A reflection that defines you is God's reflection. It's a reflection that is beyond what you see physically; rather, it is the inner and outer disposition of your relationship with God and how you portray that relationship.

> For if anyone is a hearer of the word and not a doer, he is like a man who looks intently at his natural face in a mirror. (James 1:23 ESV)

Reflecting the glory of God is about the manifestation of holiness, righteousness, trust, forgiveness, obedience, and faith. It's manifesting the fruit of the Spirit and so much more, which exemplifies the glory of God.

I fell in love with understanding God's appeasement—that it's about understanding the ways of God and understanding that his glory is as a light that can never be dimmed but instead should spread across nations.

Imagine God making me that reflection of his light after the journey of remolding and restoration. Then, by mistake or by chance, I fall short of nurturing it in the way I ought to care for it. The outcome, without a doubt, is that the light will surely diminish.

> He says: "It is too light a thing that you should be my servant to raise up the tribes of Jacob and to bring back the preserved of Israel; I will make you as a light for the nations, that my salvation may reach to the end of the earth." (Isaiah 49:6 ESV)

Reflecting the glory of God is a demonstration of the ways of God. It is attesting the truth in the Word of God. It's craving the knowledge of God always, and it's evidence of godly compassion.

THE GLORY OF HIS LIGHT OVER DARKNESS

> Arise, shine, for your light has come, and the glory of the LORD has risen upon you. For behold,

> darkness shall cover the earth, and thick darkness the peoples; but the LORD will arise upon you, and his glory will be seen upon you. And nations shall come to your light. (Isaiah 60:1–3 ESV)

I had to read this over and over: "And nations shall come to your light." Oh my! What glorious power light has over darkness! Darkness could be heartbreak; darkness could be financial setbacks. It could be physical, emotional, or spiritual repression.

Every time I shut my eyes to sleep, I see nothing, apart from blackness or my imagination. This blackness is similar to the effect of darkness. Blindness symbolizes darkness. Blindness doesn't relate to being physically disabled because there are visually disabled individuals who are more energetic than some who are physically sighted.

This view gives an easy understanding of why some prayers about spiritual eyes are synonymous with the words *spiritual blindness*. No form of darkness can be part of your likeness, once you have aligned your image to the reflector of Light, who is able to mend the brokenhearted, set captives free, and give sight to the spiritually and physically sightless. Once you have positioned your view with God's glory, you will demonstrate and exhibit that same glorious light.

> The Spirit of the Lord is on me, because he has anointed me to proclaim good news to the poor. He has sent me to proclaim freedom for the prisoners and recovery of sight for the blind, to set the oppressed free. (Luke 4:18 NIV)

Being a reflection of God's glory is like a shining light of righteousness, a magnificent light that mesmerizes a world filled with darkness by disseminating salvation and righteousness, as evidence of God's glory in us.

> For God, who said, "Light shall shine out of darkness," is the One who has shone in our hearts to give the Light of the knowledge of the glory of God in the face of Christ. (2 Corinthians 4:6 AMP)

The everyday reflection we see of ourselves in the mirror can never be collated to the replica of God we see in ourselves. The glory and power of God is a reflection that lives within us, and it is manifested through us for others to see and to have knowledge of the glory and power of God.

ATTRIBUTES OF GOD'S GLORY

For God to allow his light to reflect through us shows that he is a God of compassion and mercy. Obviously, he wouldn't want his children to be in darkness; hence, he said, "Child, I need you to clutch this light and make sure you walk in it as you go. Make sure that its luminosity enough for others to have access to it, for a lot of people are in the dark."

> Again, Jesus spoke to them, saying, "I am the light of the world. Whoever follows me will not walk-in darkness, but will have the light of life."
> (John 8:12 ESV)

The display of compassion and a heart of forgiveness is part of God's glory that every child of God should manifest. I personally exhibit and demonstrate this compassion and forgiving spirit because I reflect God, and God is a God of compassion and a God of mercy. You cannot be a reflection of God without genuinely mastering and manifesting his attributes.

> The Lord is gracious and full of compassion, slow to anger and abounding in lovingkindness. The Lord is

> good to all, and His tender mercies are over all His works. (Psalm 145:8–9 AMP)

While sitting at my work desk, a thought about the very beginning popped into my mind. It was about the word that God proclaimed into creation of man by securing man's creation with his image.

> Then God said, "Let us make man in our image, after our likeness. And let them have dominion over the fish of the sea and over the birds of the heavens and over the livestock and over all the earth and over every creeping thing that creeps on the earth." (Genesis 1:26 ESV)

I thought, *What if God isn't a merciful Father? What if he decides to wipe out humanity and all living creatures from the surface of the earth? What if God decides to revoke his significance from us after the sin of our first parents?* These questions led me to think of the time of Noah, when God had the power to destroy the earth, but instead, his compassion accorded all creatures a second chance.

I love the lyrics to "Second Chance" by Hezekiah Walker, especially the part that says:

> Lord I need to feel the touch of Your hand
> Your will for my life I want to understand
> Lord forgive me like only You can
> For you are the God of a second chance
> Lord I'm tired of the way that I am
> In Your love I want to live and stand
> To heed to Your every command
> For You're the God of a second chance
> For You're the God of a second chance

God is certainly the God of a second chance. The fact remains that God is God, and with or without our existence, he still remains

God. Because he has compassion and forgiveness, he also offers mercy. And the sweet part is that he sent his only begotten Son to put an end to the life of sin and death. Hallelujah! I feel so excited!

> Because through Christ Jesus the law of the Spirit who gives life has set you free from the law of sin and death. (Romans 8:12 NIV)

19

An Obsession beyond Ordinary Knowledge

Every time I remember my kinship with the nature of Christ, and every time I remember that everything I touch is blessed because I have the privilege of feeling God's touch in my life, and every time I remember how lucky I am to heed every command he gives me, it reassures me of my purpose in Christ.

Your life will never be the same once you understand your purpose and once you reflect on God's purpose. As a genuine child of God, the characteristics of compassion and forgiveness will always be part of your glow as a display of God's glory.

Why do I have an obsession with trusting God and obeying him? This is a question to which I have no answer. When it became an obsession, it was more of, "I can do this. I will do this," rather than, "I can't do this" or "I will not do this." And without question, the outcome of such an obsession today is visible without my expressing it in words. All along, I have felt that my trust and obedience was the result of my knowledge of God. On the other hand, this obsession came as a result of my analysis of the Word of God.

You truly understand the distinction of your spiritual growth when analyzing the Word of God, rather than the level of knowledge of the spoken words of God. Moreover, understanding these two different levels only happens when you have come to a full comprehension of who you reflect.

As I looked through the Bible during one of my trips through Heathrow Airport in England, I decided to have a little study time while waiting for my flight to arrive. As I read through the Bible, I came across the following passage:

> After breakfast Jesus asked Simon Peter, "Simon son of John, do you love me more than these?" "Yes, Lord," Peter replied, "you know I love you." "Then feed my lambs," Jesus told him. Jesus repeated the question: "Simon son of John, do you love me?" "Yes, Lord," Peter said, "you know I love you." "Then take care of my sheep," Jesus said. A third time he asked him, "Simon son of John, do you love me?" Peter was hurt that Jesus asked the question a third time. He said, "Lord, you know everything. You know that I love you." Jesus said, "Then feed my sheep." (John 21:15–17 NLT)

The tricky part about this passage, for me, is that I knew about the words that were said to Peter just by reading through this scripture, but there is more understanding to this scripture and what was said to Peter.

It is so easy to read a scripture and digest it, but how do you show that scripture into an exhibit with its original theory? Reading and understanding this passage exemplifies for me the meaning of analyzing the Word of God. My analysis of this scripture is that Jesus could have asked the question and said what he had to say just once, but he asked Simon Peter the same question three times because he needed Peter to understand that what he was saying was beyond understanding; it was about analyzing what Jesus was saying.

In our modern times, a lot of young people often use the

phrase "I love you" without having action attached to it. You can't blame such individuals because they are examples of misplaced understanding.

Jesus putting a question to Peter three times and emphasizing what he wanted him to do three times was beyond the point of acknowledgement; rather, it was in the direction of accomplishment.

AN UNDERSTANDING OF HEARING AND STUDYING HIS GLORY, JUST BY HIS HEARTBEAT

While still reading the scripture of John 21, I heard a boarding call and looked up to check the screen to see if it was my flight. As I raised my eyes, a young boy caught my attention. He was whining and pleading with his mum to get him something, tugging on her hands as he led her in the direction of what he wanted. Being a short distance from them, all I could see was his mouth saying, "Mama, please. Mama, please."

Seeing this mother-and-son performance at the airport made me smile. I remembered that every time my son wanted something from me, he would walk up to me with a sweet face and say, "Mummy, you are so beautiful."

I would smile and say, "Thank you, baby."

And then he'd say, "Mummy do you love me?"

I would answer the obvious, "Yes, I do."

And then he'd say, "Mum, I need you to..."

And the rest is history because he knew without doubt that I would fall for it. It's actually an approach that I have studied, so even without him completing his statement, I would respond with a yes or a no to his request.

Jesus needed Peter to do something for him, and this was why he threw a question to Peter with the elucidation aimed at the fact that Peter's level of understanding Jesus should have been beyond knowledge or listening. Rather, it should have been on a level of understanding Jesus's heartbeat, a level of understanding that loving him was beyond Peter's saying, "I do love you, Master." Rather, it was about the action of Peter's professed love of Jesus. Such indulgence is on the magnitude of liaising with God through the heart. It is simply a point of hearing and studying God's heartbeat, even without him speaking. This type of understanding is identical to understanding your own name. It's an understanding with the rationale that your reflection is aligned with trust and obedience. It's an understanding of knowing that the more you obey, the more you have power. Once you acquire this power from God through your obedience, there is no turning back.

Who wouldn't want to be a reflection of a glory that never fades? The type of glory that surpasses anything and everything; the type of glory that is hopeful, even in the midst of impediments; the type of glory that can never be compared. No, God's glory can never be shared. He said,

> I am the Lord; that is my name! I will not yield my glory to another or my praise to idols.
> (Isaiah 42:8 NIV)

I now understand why my hope in God is this audaciously firm. I could just call it a godly hope. And this is from the justification that I am a reflection of an increased glory. Yippee!

Reflecting on God's glory is a demonstration of trusting him. It's a demonstration of knowing that the mere reflection you see in your mirror can never be compared to God's reflection.

> Delight yourself in the Lord, and he will give you the desires of your heart. Commit your way to the Lord; trust in him, and he will act. He will bring forth your righteousness as the light, and your justice as the noonday. (Psalm 37:4–6 ESV)

Trusting God is putting his nature and character on display. Once you are obedient, you will trust, and once your trust is endowed, then trusting God, with no atom of hesitation, is the act of proclaiming his glory.

MANIFESTING HIS POWER THROUGH HIS PURPOSE

Our life's motive should be reflecting the glory of God in all we do. It shouldn't just be a veneer; we should be able to keep the flame burning without halting. Having an endless flame in you that is the reflection of Christ will flare up his demonstrative power in you with all understanding.

The manifestation of God's power is knowing that your thoughts and your actions must be aligned with God's view. You cannot be a reflection of God and still dwell on the notion of fear or on the notion of accomplishments and all that life generally throws in your face. It can't work that way. Always remember that it's not the world's display that you are reflecting, but it's the display of Christ. Because you reflect Christ, that means once he says, "You can do all things through me who strengthens you," that means you can actually do it.

> I can do all things through Christ who strengthens me. (Philippians 4:13 KJV)

My life became expurgated from the minute I saw myself distinctively and understood that it is not me who dwells in me, but it is Christ who dwells in me.

> In that day you will know that I am in My Father, and you in Me, and I in you. (John 14:20 ESV)

In the past, there was a time when I might have lost sleep over what people said, but truth is the glory and power I reflect now; it's too immoderate for me to fret over it. Being in my field of vision right now is enough for you to eradicate any form of shame from your past; any value or lack of value in your physical looks; any unrealistic, self-inflicted standards that are yet to be attained or might never be attained. Once your entity is aimed 100 percent through the reflection of Christ, you will have a satisfactory heart, even in an atmosphere of emptiness, because now you know that you can trust God to accomplish all that he is willing to do.

> Now to him who is able to do immeasurably more than all we ask or imagine, according to his power that is at work within us, to him be glory in the church and in Christ Jesus throughout all generations, forever and ever! Amen. (Ephesians 3:20–21 NIV)

20

Functioning with Purpose

Be focused. Being a reflection of God's glory is being a reflection of Christ.

> Jesus answered, "I am the way and the truth and the life. No one comes to the Father except through me." (John 14:6 NIV)

As my Australian sisters would say, the *dinkum oil* (which means "the truth") is that God sees you in Christ, and once you are seen in Christ, you need to be holy."

Holiness is the only condition of seeing your true identity and reflection. Your focus should be for the reason of God's perspective of you, which is holiness.

> But just as he who called you is holy, so be holy in all you do. (1 Peter 1:15 NIV)

WALKING WITH GOD

Walking with God is a wonderful and unique way of life. It is a journey of purpose. It is a walk of love and obedience to the fulfillment of our purpose in life.

To everyone God has called and those who have truly been on this walk with God, you will appreciate that God reveals himself in phases through some difficult experiences we go through in life.

God reveals himself to us, depending on our level of understanding of our spiritual assignments.

When we look at the progression of our spiritual growth, we can understand that as we get closer to God, we tend to understand him more and more. We no longer know him through our parents or pastors, reading someone's journal, or hearing the experiences of others. We have an encounter with our Lord Jesus Christ himself. That is, we begin to manifest the fruits of the Spirit, especially the fruit of patience on the journey.

> But the Holy Spirit produces this kind of fruit in our lives: love, joy, peace, patience, kindness, goodness, faithfulness. (Galatians 5:22 NLT)

Walking with God is an exhilarating journey. Your vision in Christ means that you have taken a ride on this unique and beautiful journey. I wish I could transfer the feeling in me since I started walking with God or display it on this page so you could understand the beauty that comes with the realization that this walk is not just any type of walk or fellowship but a walk of love. It's a walk of obedience. One of the most rewarding aspects about this type of walk is knowing that it is for the fulfilment of a purposeful life.

One of my obligations during the season of rebranding with Christ was with one of my mentees. As odd as this would have been, it was one of those seasons when I realized that I am totally in Christ.

It was a long one with her, as she was someone who would be

fully attentive one minute, but in the next minute, she would do something opposite from the directives. The compassion of Christ that I had in me guided me, and it became that strength of patience I needed to complete my purpose with her. I understood that my relationship with this mentee was beyond the school environment, and I strongly knew that she was God's, sent for a cause. I could not place the purpose initially outside the regular training ground—not until I got a clear vision of my assignment. That was when I knew that she was actually a broken piece.

There were times when I could have given up on her or could have said, "You know what? I'm done." But every time such overwhelming thoughts came to me, I would get a reminder of my calling and my purpose. One day, I became strained because it seemed that my words were bouncing back over and over with regard to a delicate subject matter.

When I got to this breaking point, I excused myself. Looking up at the ceiling, I took a deep breath, paused, and asked myself, "Is this really worth it? This young lady is getting me so worked up." At the same time that I was questioning myself, I experienced a calm breeze of words that cleansed my thought of giving up on her:

"If I have embraced you over every difficult experience and have given you this grace to mold and carry people along, then you will dare not to give up on this assignment. Do you know that giving up on this young lady is giving up on the reason I sent her to you in the first place? My child, I have given you the strength on this one. Trust me; for this one, you will remold her just as I remolded you."

Smiling at these words, I saw myself in a reflective glass in my office and said to myself, "I reflect God. If he can do it, then his reflection will do it."

Today, that young lady is a mentor herself. Once you remember who you truly reflect, rest assured that God will always reveal himself in all levels of understanding to those who are called and who are in true fellowship with him. He knows that we always need that closeness for the progression of our spiritual growth.

REFLECTING THE TIMELESS ZONE

Understanding our reflection in God is understanding him more and more. And understanding him more and more is understanding what it means and how it feels to take a side-by-side walk of liberty with the Son of God, which comes with so much manifestation of his power.

This understanding comes with the fact that God has a way of revealing himself in unimaginable ways. It could be through difficult experiences in our personal lives, our work lives, our emotional lives, our financial lives, or life in general.

I have been there, my dear friend, and I am still there. No form of attainment in life can be compared with this freedom and the unrestrained access that I have with Christ. I am a reflection of Christ because I see myself in Christ, and, for this, I automatically became a reflection of his splendor and power. I have irresistibly become evidence of his Word, and I am a full reflection of his timeless zone, which is an eternal zone.

Once you see yourself in Christ, know that you have stepped into a timeless zone, which means that you are also a timeless zone. This is because of the truth that you are a reflection of the one who is timeless, who is called Christ the Lord.

Imagine being a reflection of the one whose existence is eternal, the one who doesn't consider time to do what he says he will do and when he says he will do it.

Time is dysfunctional to Christ because he doesn't regard time to say what he has to say, and he doesn't even affix time to his supremacy. He can decide to change time and any season at his command, so imagine being a reflection of this wondrous God, who holds the bearing of time in his palm. Oh, hallelujah!

As a reflector of Christ, all we need to have is the genuine understanding of who Christ is. As a true reflector of Christ, we should know that Christ that dwells in us and will always be outside of time. Let's fasten our eyes on the prize of a crown that can only be given to us by the one who is our true reflection.

> And the Word became flesh and dwelt among us, and we have seen his glory, glory as of the only Son from the Father, full of grace and truth. (John 1:14 ESV)

FUNCTIONING WITH PURPOSE

The beautiful me that I never saw had to deal with change. It reached a point where I had to be on standby, in the guise of spiritual hibernation, for my reinvention.

And this time, I was at a totally different observation level of my reinvention. I looked beyond the physical. I looked beyond what I saw in the mirror. It was more like a reflection beyond the surface. It was a deeper view. It was more of a concave scrutiny. It was an inward observation. Then a thoughtful question popped into my mind: *What's your level of functionality?*

For us to function with purpose, we need to pause or stand by.

For us to function with purpose, we need a big change—a win-win change.

For us to function with purpose, we need to fall into a place of hibernation. Once we are hibernating, we will be ready for reinvention.

Every process it took to unearth my beauty within was worth it. It's a beautiful thing to grasp God's hallmark. If you have yet to grasp God's standard, please recalibrate inwardly, and you will see beyond the physical.

To understand your purpose, ask yourself this: "What suits me?" and "Where's my place with God?" Once you have an answer to those questions, your experience will become your currency, where there are no impediments.

Discovering your beauty within is attached to your purpose on earth, which brings about true knowledge. It is a confidence-builder and a reaping of the merit of fulfilment for yourself and the God who created you.

Once you are identified with this type of beauty, you can never be short of contentment. Your peak of livelihood, creativity, re-creation, discernment, multiplication, and fulfillment becomes royalty, like your Father in heaven.

> Whoever says he abides in him ought to walk in the same way in which he walked. (1 John2:6 ESV)

Cease consternation, complaints, and competition, as you are now grounded with confidence, insight, and intuition.

Your beauty that lives within is a place of resurfacing. You stop existing and start living the purposeful life of your rebirth. Your life then becomes a life where it's not a directive of your voice but a place where all that is heard is God's voice.

PURSUIT OF PURPOSE

Think about it: negative experiences we had in the past, which were blown out of proportion because of fear and ignorance of the promise of God in our lives, affected our mindsets of who we are in Christ.

The scriptures tell us, "We are a royal priesthood in Christ, a chosen generation" (1 Peter 2:9 KJV).

There is so much more that can be said about who we are in Christ. This reality is inexhaustible. It is according to God's riches in glory, my Christ Jesus. It is unfathomable.

You have a duty to yourself, as a new creation believer in Christ, to know by experience who you are in Him.

There are no ready-made libraries of experiences or archive sites for the things you endured to get to where you are today, emotionally. I used to jokingly say that some of the things we have been through are experiences; it's only God who can reward us. No human effort can adequately recompense us to measure up with what we may have had to go though.

A human being born of a woman can understand enough, so that so there is no need to expect that from anyone. That is why our focus in life should be on fulfilling our purpose on earth.

Some difficult and painful situations may have affected some of our relationships, to the point where we were defined wrongly, misrepresented, and so much more.

Our Lord Jesus Chris said,

> I tell you the truth, unless a kernel of wheat is planted in the soil and dies, it remains alone. But it's death will produce many new kernel—a plentiful harvest of new lives. (John 12:24 NLT)

Until we lay down the wounds we have from the journey of the pursuit of purpose for Jesus to heal us of our natural emotions, we will not be delivered of that I-deserve-better mindset or submit to his will.

Think of Joseph and all he had to go through. How could an ex-convict become a prime minister of a great nation?

God is about to release record-breakers and mold-breakers across the earth. God is about to shake tables and pull down mountains through the most unusual and unique individuals—those who have been through experiences and have lived to tell the stories.

As I progressed through that season of growth, through the pain of my father's death, God assured me that all things work together for good for those who believe. The Lord explained to me that it was not about being broken but beautiful. It was not about who was better; it was about who was ready to carry the cross and follow him.

When a call is made, everyone hears it; everyone also answers, but not everyone wants to go the extra mile. That's the reason I said to you, "Come up more." Not everyone believes they should sacrifice their all. Coming up more is a sacrifice born out of love that means you should persevere.

When you stay a bit longer, it becomes easy to forget where you have come from and all you have been through and to focus on why you are there and the glory that awaits you.

The reward of this level of sacrifice is love, as you will learn to love like Christ did. With so much revelation, you tend to see what no one has seen, heard, or imagined because of the privilege—you are allowed by God to see the glory.

You will begin to have more knowledge, information, grace, responsibility, understanding, and to love more than before.

Look at Elijah—he knew that where he was going was much better than where he was, so he gave Elisha his mantle.

When you are equipped with knowledge and information, it brings confidence and love—if we are truly devoted Christians who have come up from the place of death and sacrifice.

21

Broken but Beautiful

Being broken but beautiful is when we exhibit love, compassion, empathy, and forgiveness, as these characteristics are the foundation of true Christianity that Christ talked about. True Christianity—no more, no less. When we have this embedded in us, then we have come up to the mountaintop. When we are driven by purpose, we have love, compassion, or forgiveness, as life is full of offense.

Christ rose and ascended, but we are humans, so we remain on the mountain. Mountains can represent our source of power or dignity, our boundaries, or the limits we have set around us. When we get to and stay in this place, we do not fight our battles; God fights our battles for us, and this is where we hold our peace. This is the time we watch God, as Abraham held his peace and provided.

LIVING FROM THE MOUNTAINTOP WITH GOD

At this point, we're actually dead, so we don't even care what happens, provided it is OK with God. Here, we are happy being alone with God, which is enmity with the world. We have a lot of enemies we don't know because we are so focused on doing the things of the Lord. At this point, we listen more than we pray because it is governed or ruled by instructions.

It is not a human realm but spiritual. At this place, we tend to listen more with fear and respect because we can't take the next step without God. It's unfamiliar terrain. God provides just enough light for the step we're on, but we have to trust him and walk in obedience and humility to his leading. Then he illuminates the next step we are to take.

In going up, not listening is a costly mistake. At this point, we will meditate more because the Lord speaks to our imagination. The Lord becomes more creative with our minds. The creative ability of God is duplicated in us at this level. This is the reason why we can heal and receive healing because we believe the impossible. Even if we drink poison, it will not hurt us. Even when a decree is made against us, it will not come to pass, as in the case of Daniel.

This level is where we become like Christ. Christ died on the cross and fulfilled his purpose. When we get to this level and die on the cross, we remain dead and start fulfilling our purpose on earth. Now, as humans, we are imperfect and prone to mistakes, errors, and sin. How can we remain dead? That is the reason for reiterating that it is a lonely and painful place to be, and only a few people can stay here. People come and go, but staying here is constant.

> Then Jesus said to his disciples, "Whoever wants to be my disciple must deny themselves and take up their cross and follow me." (Matthew 16:24 NIV)

The "come hither" we speak of isn't one of partial deadness to self. You must be willing, with a sincere hunger, to serve God and be ready to go all the way with Christ and to walk into the newness of another level. While leaving family behind and all things that easily lure you back, remember that God may give you a vision or speak a word that others don't hear, so don't expect them to run with you. Be willing and ready to go alone.

> Because we understand our fearful responsibility to the Lord, we work hard to persuade others. (2 Corinthians 5:11–12 NLT)

Broken but Beautiful has discussed the true beauty of a child of God. Having done all to stand, stand, therefore.

It's about the beauty that lies within.

Beauty is in the eye of the beholder.

When your beauty complements your purpose on earth, then you are truly beautiful. It is written:

> He has made everything beautiful in its time. (Ecclesiastes 3:11 NIV)

Beloved of God, the most important revelation you need at this time is to know that your season and the time to be unstoppable—in every aspect of your life where you have stepped out as a believer to do things—has come! When the time comes for restoration, restitution, and manifestation of reward, seasons will converge to carry out the assignments of God on behalf of his children.

Becoming foolish for God will make you beautiful before men.

You don't have to defend your action because people will not understand it when God is building your character.

You don't have to be cool and calculated when you're breaking barriers.

God is never late. He knows what we don't know and sees what we can never see in our lifetimes.

Have you ever had pain that made you complain, cry, or vent to someone else and get counseling, comforting, or a solution?

What about the pain that numbed you?

Have you been deprived of power; unable to think, feel, or respond normally; or in a state of shock?

This type of pain was meant to break your will and desire. They are meant for you to bear alone; this kind of pain creates a vacuum that causes you to appreciate God, the Holy Spirit. Only God can fill that vacuum.

This kind is meant to reveal to you the true nature of human beings. It is to expand you; it is for spiritual delivery to show you that you were nothing but a mere human. It's to change you and challenge your status quo.

God is the only one at work here. It's your walk with God alone.

The previous challenges you went through were your work with destiny-helpers, but the pain's numbing is meant for you to meditate. It is meant to give you a personal encounter and to deal with purpose. It's a one-on-one class with your Creator.

In this place of total surrender to your God, your experience becomes personal and different; that's why you're quiet and separated. (See Matthew 17:1–3.) The transfiguration reflects a separation in different levels: change, glory, sanctification, total obedience, submission, sacrifice.

This brings you to a place of confidence, confirmation, victory, and reflecting the glory of God in your life.

> For all creation is waiting eagerly for that future day when God will reveal who his children really are. (Romans 8:19 NLT)

Here, you know the voice of God. No need to pretend because of revelation knowledge, vision, promises, testimonies, and witnesses.

If you pretend not to hear God, it's probably because you want to rebel or live in denial. It is often not what you want, so you ignore his nudges, dreams, and revelations, hoping he will change his mind, or you might be unsure.

At this point, you come to terms with the reality of being a Christian. God will not budge for you—either you go back, remain where you are, or go forward. The only way is his way, and you will know the truth that will set you free.

Lightning Source UK Ltd.
Milton Keynes UK
UKHW040624150223
416722UK00034B/908/J

9 781664 254701